England's Moon

CRXSO

*Saint Helena's Place in the History of
Modern Science Fiction*

David J. Jeremiah

England's Moon

'It seemeth to be an earthly Paradise.'

JAN HUIGEN VAN LINSCHOTEN, *HIS DISCOURS OF VOYAGES INTO YE EASTE & WEST INDIES*, 1598

'... this cursed rock...'

NAPOLEON BONAPARTE, ON FIRST SEEING SAINT HELENA IN 1815

'A Plantation, sent out years since by its metropolitan Planet...'

THOMAS PYNCHON, *MASON & DIXON*, 1997

ALSO BY DAVID J. JEREMIAH
Shakespeare's Island: Saint Helena and *The Tempest*

Contents

England's Moon

Acknowledgements

Anyone who writes a book will owe a great deal to others: previous authors, librarians, family members and many more. Isaac Newton, in an uncharacteristic outbreak of modesty, wrote that his achievements were attributable to being able to stand on the shoulders of giants. I hope that my debt to other writers, giants included, is sufficiently acknowledged in the bibliography, notes and references that I have included.

Libraries still have a place, even in the age of the internet. I have been particularly reliant on the British Library and the Public Library in Jamestown, Saint Helena, which is home to a number of works that are hard to find elsewhere. The Saint Helena Archives have also proved to be something of a treasure chest of information. I thank the staff of all of these institutions for their courtesy and assistance. My wife, Joy, has, as always, been unfailingly supportive and at times has persuaded me to persevere when I doubted that I would complete the task: writing a book is not as easy as some authors are able to make it appear.

Basil and Barbara George helped me with a great deal of information, including the location of what remains of the Ladder Hill Observatory and of the Magnetical and Meteorological Observatory at Longwood. Michael Benjamin showed me the antique clocks at Plantation House and Peter Williams took the time and trouble to accompany me there in order to explain how he maintains them in working order. The staff and volunteers at the Saint Helena Museum assisted me in a number of respects, including with items in the museum's collection that are not on public display. Thank you to Stedson Stroud M.B.E., whose work on Saint Helena's sister island of Ascension caused me to write Chapter Eight and who was kind enough to meet with me and answer a number of questions about it.

Finally, a thank you to my editor, Anna Buckett, for her patience and guidance. Any errors that remain are entirely my own.

Preface

Small inhabited islands have a strange hold over people: complete in themselves they seem to offer an opportunity to know everything that can be known about a place and its people. New arrivals can quickly come to regard themselves as experts – proposing everything from government reforms to the planting of new species. The reality is that small islands do not give up their secrets easily and are as complex, if not more so, than much larger places. It is always wise to keep in mind that things may be as they are because it suits those who live there.

Saint Helena is about the same size as Jersey, the largest of the Channel Islands. In almost all other respects it is very different. Viewed from the sea, Saint Helena presents itself as a single rock, looming large out of the South Atlantic. It quickly rises to over 2,700 feet, in the form of Diana's Peak, and its considerable distance from anywhere else makes it remarkable: the nearest other land is Ascension Island, more than seven hundred miles to its north-west, and the closest point in Africa is over twelve hundred miles away to the east. Ascension Island is even smaller than Saint Helena, at only 34 square miles.

Saint Helena's history is traced in this book over a period of more than five hundred years. Because of its remoteness, its human story has a clear starting point: it remained undiscovered, in the strict sense of that word, until 1502, when a Portuguese fleet returning from India came across it. No human eyes had seen it before.

The Portuguese did not colonise the island, leaving it as a place where ships could take on water, supplementing this natural resource by releasing goats and planting fruit trees, which provided both meat and the vital vitamin C that was necessary to combat scurvy. They built a church in what is now Jamestown, known for many years as Chapel Valley, but discouraged settlement. Sailors left onshore to recover from shipborne ailments would be picked up by vessels calling later at the island, if they were lucky enough to revive and survive.

The Dutch made a claim of sorts to the island in 1633 but left nobody there to sustain and protect it, which left Saint Helena free to be settled by the English East India Company in 1659. Its history thereafter was that of 'John Company' until 1834, when it became a Crown possession, which it remains today. Saint Helena is one of the fourteen remnants of empire known as the United Kingdom Overseas Territories.

The island's principal settlement is Jamestown. It is a gem, reminiscent of an English seaside town in Devon or Dorset, with mostly eighteenth and early nineteenth century buildings, some with wrought iron balconies overlooking Main Street, the principal thoroughfare. The four hundred yards or so that Main Street extends over seem like a fragment of the England that many who came to live on the island, from Africa, India, China and elsewhere, had never seen, uniquely presented in the remoteness of the South Atlantic.

A visitor approaching the town from the sea enters after crossing an impressively deep and waterless moat and then passing under an arch set in the town wall. Beyond this there is a castle, the origins of which date back to the seventeenth century, when it was known as Saint John's Fort. The considerable expanse of the Parade then opens up, now largely used as a car park. On the left is the entrance to the Castle, which is still the seat of the island's administration, with which it is synonymous. Uphill of this is the Police Office, as it will always be called by islanders however many times it is renamed. The force's headquarters is now located in Upper Jamestown. There is also the Law Court, with its ceremonial staves dating from the reign of William IV, whose coat of arms is still fixed in position above the judicial chair. Immediately beyond the Court is the Public Library. Entering the library through its front entrance I always cast my eyes to the right, where there is a suitably antique book case, glass fronted and locked. It is the main reason I go there: it contains a collection of books about the island, some of which are over two hundred years old. A staff member produces the key and I settle down for a good read. On one of my many visits, thinking myself to know as much as most about the island's past, I selected *Saint Helena Britannica*, a collection of the writings of the late Trevor Hearl, a tireless collector of information about Saint Helena.[1] Chapter 1 of *Saint Helena Britannica* is headed *The Age of Discovery and St Helena's 'Man in the Moon'*. I read on. How had I not known about Saint Helena's connection with a seventeenth century work of science fiction? The idea for this book was born. It would be interesting to learn more about this early work, but what if Saint Helena had also

---

[1] Hearl died in 2007 and his papers are now kept at the Bodleian Library, University of Oxford.

inspired other works in this popular category of literature? There was a great deal left to discover.

Introduction

Science fiction, one might reasonably think, is simply fiction with a significant element of science in it, although controversy rages over what falls within this apparently self-evident definition: the result being that the line between it and other genres is often blurred. It may be difficult to completely pin it down as a subject but most of us know it when we see it. I have not been overly prescriptive in this regard, including in this book subjects such as fantasy and alternative history, both of which are accepted by many as sub-genres of science fiction, although they may at times have little obvious science in them.

The term 'Science-Fiction' was coined in 1851 by William Wilson in *A Little Earnest Book Upon a Great Old Subject*, to describe a book written the previous year – *The Poor Artist: Or Seven Eye-Sights and One Object*. The author of *The Poor Artist*, R.H. Horne, had addressed the question of how different creatures (including humans) may perceive a single object in different ways. The science of this is in the state of knowledge at the time of how the eyes of different creatures work. But there is also the philosophical question of how much is actually seen and how much is simply fulfilling the pre-programmed expectation of the observer. What is in our 'mind's eye' is a theme dating back to at least Chaucer's *The Man of Law's Tale*, written in 1387. In Horne's book, the artist of the title attempts to reduce to pictorial form what a bee, an ant, a spider, a fish, a cat, and a robin describe to him as he rests in a 'half-wakeful condition' in a wood. The seventh creature is himself. The object that each of the others tells the artist of is a bright sovereign. They then lead the artist to this, which he uses to cover the cost of putting his paintings on public display. The exhibition is largely a failure: people know what they like, and they want pictures of their prize bulls, country homes and other things that they are familiar with, depicted as they see them. Persuaded by his wife to accept this reality the artist goes on to make his fortune, giving people what they want to see. But it was the science in the book that caught the imagination of William Wilson when he published his *A Little Earnest Book* the following year, in which he wrote:

> Fiction has lately been chosen as a means of familiarizing science in one single case only, but with great success. It is by the celebrated dramatic Poet, R. H. Horne, and is entitled "The Poor Artist; or, Seven Eye-Sights and One Object." We hope it will not be long before we may have other works of Science-Fiction, as we believe such books likely to fulfil a good purpose, and create an interest, where, unhappily, science alone might fail.'[1]

In short, science alone might seem dull or difficult to many of us but fictionalisation of it may cause readers to think about it a bit more. An entertaining book may prove to be more enlightening 'as a means of familiarizing science' than a formal work on the subject, which many of us may be reluctant to take down from the bookshelf anyway. Certainly, the works that I have read while writing this book have had Wilson's desired effect on me: I had little previous interest in such things as pursuit curves, terraforming, the lunar-distance method and the finer points of magnetic variation.

---

[1] P. 137.

But science fiction as a subject for writers did not simply arrive on the scene in the mid-nineteenth century, until then it simply lacked a name. Here another debate begins. Regardless of when the genre was given its modern description, when did it first emerge as a literary form? To some, the search goes back several thousand years, to ancient civilisations and their stories. But fable and fantasy, it is argued by others, lack an essential element: there is nothing seriously scientific, for example, about a ride on a magic carpet. It is magic that science fiction left behind when it became a genre in its own right. No longer would strange occurrences and natural phenomena be explained only in terms of religious or other traditional beliefs. Apparently impossible-to-believe stories could be written on the basis that there might well be rational explanations of them: with science, however speculative, providing answers that could render them plausible.

I have chosen to limit the parameters of this book to science fiction (broadly defined) in the context of an island only 47 miles square in the South Atlantic, the island of Saint Helena. To this extent I have made my task both easier and more difficult: easier in the sense that historians of science fiction frequently complain that the subject is too large to manage within the confines of a single book, and more difficult because a reader may take some persuading that a small island in such a remote location can possibly have had a sufficient impact on the development of modern science fiction to warrant a book of its own on the subject.

The early history of Saint Helena coincides with what are generally referred to as the Age of Discovery and the Age of Reason, each of which had a profound effect on what was available to authors to be written about. A much larger world became known to Europeans as voyagers began increasingly to undertake oceanic expeditions.

The Azores, over a thousand miles west of Lisbon, were located by the Portuguese as early as the fourteenth century, but exploration in earnest came a century or more later. In parallel with this the study of science came of age. Taken together, these led to the development of modern science fiction. If there was still so much to be discovered about our own planet what might there be left to find elsewhere in the universe? As voyagers explored the world, astronomers set about exploring the heavens – observing, and speculating about, what might be found there. A flight to the Moon might be the stuff of fiction, but even without travelling there it could be studied in some detail with the aid of a telescope, a tool invented in the early seventeenth century. As with the gradually unravelling Earth, the Moon could be mapped and features on it given names. It could be regarded as a new world of its own and, in common with recently discovered places on Earth, the Moon and the planets might well have potential as colonies.

Travel narratives of the period often read like science fiction. They frequently merged fiction with fact and in many instances writers were less than diligent in ensuring that it was fact that predominated. Even without embellishment, accounts of exotic peoples and places could seem as unreal to many readers as a fictional description of a visit to the Moon. Truth was often stranger than fiction and on occasion it was fiction that might be the more convincing of the two. The finding of a unicorn's horn (Queen Elizabeth I received a gift of what was said to be one) seemed more plausible than reports of creatures that actually existed. When the preserved corpse of a duck-billed platypus (*Ornithorhynchus anatinus*) was made available to scientists in 1799 it was regarded as a hoax, with parts of different creatures thought to have been assembled together for the purpose. Who could take seriously a mammal that laid eggs? Science and science fiction have in common that they both require an open mind.

But open minds were regarded as something of a threat to established beliefs, particularly in the area of religion. One of the things that struck me as I wrote this book was how many of those who feature in it were clergymen. In Elizabethan and Jacobean England, and for some time thereafter, the best educated members of society were those heading for a career in the church. Until the Reformation this had been the main purpose of taking a degree at Oxford or Cambridge (which remained the only English universities until the 1820s) and the legacy of this lived on. Typically, progress towards ordination would commence with a Bachelor of Arts degree, which offered a general education, including the classics, history and geography. Francis Godwin, who is given some prominence in this book, provides an example. He took his Bachelor's degree in 1581, his Master of Arts in 1584, and successively thereafter the degrees of Bachelor and Doctor of Divinity. The consequence of this system of higher education was that those best placed to question biblical teaching were those least able to do so if they wished to keep their jobs. There were important questions to answer which it might be unwise for a priest to confront. Did the Genesis account of the Creation rule out any question of evolution here on Earth? Was Earth the only populated planet? Where was Heaven to be found in a universe increasingly explored and laid bare by the telescope? Science fiction offered a way of examining difficult ideas without necessarily putting them forward as one's own beliefs.

Francis Godwin was Bishop of Hereford when he wrote *The Man in the Moone*, which is generally considered to be the earliest science fiction novel written in English. Probably because of his position, he chose not to publish the book during his own lifetime. But tolerance of science by the church was moving forward, albeit slowly. A twenty-four year old clergyman, John Wilkins, later to become a bishop himself, published his *The Discovery of a World in the Moone: or, A Discourse Tending to Prove, That 'Tis Probable There May Be Another Habitable World in That Planet* in 1638, the same year that *The Man in the Moone* finally appeared. Wilkins chose to confront rather than avoid the issue, arguing the theological case for publishing a work that could be considered by some to be blasphemous. He suggested that the idea of an inhabited Moon, 'doth not contradict any principle of reason or faith.' As David Cressy has put it, 'The year

1638 could well be considered England's Lunar moment'.[2] Wilkins' book and the posthumously published *Man in the Moone* of Francis Godwin went to print within a few months of each other. Wilkins was much impressed by the rival work and revised his own accordingly.

Adam Roberts has argued in his *The History of Science Fiction* that the 'science fiction imagination'[3] emerged as a part of Western Protestant culture, which was perhaps more tolerant than the Roman Catholic Church in its response to scientific advance. Nevertheless, even in Protestant England, care was still required by those who chose to write about science, factual or fictional. Beyond Godwin's time, Edmond Halley was denied preferment to the post of Savilian Professor of Astronomy at Oxford University in 1691, following the opposition to his appointment by the then Archbishop of Canterbury, John Tillotson, acting together with Edward Stillingfleet, the Bishop of Worcester. Tillotson and Stillingfleet based their opposition to Halley's appointment on his lack of orthodoxy in religious matters.

As late as the nineteenth century, Charles Darwin, who had once been destined for a career in the Church,[4] was taken to task by prominent Christians for similar reasons, although in his case he had largely brought this upon himself. By 1849 he had taken to Sunday strolls rather than attending church with his family. He confessed in 1879 to at least being an agnostic, a word coined only ten years previously.[5] Surprisingly, none of this prevented his burial in Westminster Abbey in 1882. The President of the Royal Society made a request for this and the Dean of Westminster, who was in France at the time, readily agreed. He later wrote: 'I did not hesitate as to my answer and telegraphed direct … that my assent would be cheerfully given.' It seems that religion and science had become reconciled. The

---

[2] *Early Modern Space Travel and the English Man in the Moon*, p. 967.

[3] P. xii.

[4] He went to Cambridge with this in mind.

[5] By T. H. Huxley, at a meeting of the Metaphysical Society that year. It is derived from the Greek word for 'unknowable'.

Bishop of Carlisle, Harvey Goodwin, delivered a memorial sermon in the Abbey on the Sunday following Darwin's funeral, in which he preached:

> 'I think that the interment of the remains of Mr Darwin in Westminster Abbey is in accordance with the judgement of the wisest of his countrymen...it would have been unfortunate if anything had occurred to give weight and currency to the foolish notion which some have diligently propagated, but for which Mr Darwin was not responsible, that there is a necessary conflict between a knowledge of Nature and a belief in God...'[6]

Bishop Goodwin was it seems prepared on behalf of the Church to move forward in ideas of what could be properly explored by a Christian. Science, as far as he was concerned, was not in conflict with faith.

Even prior to this, Westminster Abbey appears to have been a place of reconciliation in such matters. When Sir Charles Lyell, the quite literally ground breaking geologist, was interred there in 1875, A.P. Stanley, who delivered the funeral address, observed: 'The tranquil triumph of Geology once thought so dangerous, now so quietly accepted by the Church, no less by the world, is one more proof of the groundlessness of theological panics in the face of the advances of scientific thought.'

---

[6] Cited by Nigel Scotland, *Darwin and the Response of the Victorian Churches*, 1986.

I
The Man in the Moone

As we have seen above, *The Man in the Moone*, first published in 1638, has a reasonable claim to be the earliest science fiction novel written in English. It tells of a flying machine, built on Saint Helena, which eventually carries its inventor to the Moon. Its author was Francis Godwin, the Bishop of Hereford from 1617 until his death in 1633.

Born in 1562, at Hannington, Northamptonshire, Godwin was a contemporary of Shakespeare. Surviving the famous poet and playwright by a considerable margin Godwin lived through the reigns of Elizabeth I, James I (James VI of Scotland) and well into that of Charles I. It follows that he experienced a time of considerable change, not least in relation to significant advances in scientific thought.

Godwin's father, Thomas Godwin, was the Bishop of Bath and Wells and it seems to have been assumed that Francis would follow Thomas into the Church. As his career developed, Francis proceeded through livings in Somerset to appointment as sub-dean of Exeter in 1587 and became Bishop of Llandaff in 1601. A surviving portrait of Godwin dating from 1613, prior to his promotion to the more prestigious and richer diocese of Hereford, is intended to impress rather than necessarily offer us a close likeness of him. He is shown with a beard, trained and trimmed in the fashion of the time, and the elegant and pale fingers of a man not much used to working with his hands. His bulky ecclesiastical robes, complete with padded sleeves, give him an imposing physical appearance, said by some to be indicative of a certain corpulence, although the depiction of his face seems to show otherwise.

Godwin was a published author during his own lifetime, perhaps best known for his *A Catalogue of the Bishops of England*. The *Catalogue* was an appropriate subject for a cleric and it assisted his advancement within the church, first bringing him appointment as Bishop of Llandaff and eventually the richer prize of Hereford, which he succeeded to in 1617. He wrote on non-ecclesiastical subjects as well and was a noted antiquary; but science, as we have seen, was a subject that required a bishop to be cautious. The consensus among scholars is that *The Man in the Moone* would not have been considered at the time to be a suitable book for a bishop to have written: some of its content could all too easily have been regarded as heretical, running contrary, as it did, to a literal reading of the Bible. This was dangerous stuff. There had been a burning at the stake for heresy as recently as 1612, the unfortunate fate of a Baptist, Edward Wightman, at Lichfield, Staffordshire on 11 April that year. The risk to Godwin's reputation, or a still worse outcome, probably explains why *The Man in the Moone* was not published until after his death: even then it appeared without attribution to him, perhaps in deference to both his posthumous reputation and to the fortunes of family members still pursuing careers in the Church. But a book written and initially kept from the eyes of others gives rise to the question of why it was written at all.

The Man in the Moone contains an exhortation to the Crown to settle Saint Helena:

'I cannot but wonder, that our King in his Wisdome hath not thought fit to plant a Colony, and to fortifie in it, being a place so necessary for refreshing of all travaillers out of the Indies, so as it is hardly possible to make a Voyage thence, without touching there.'[1]

It would hardly have been possible to gain support for this proposal without there being some way that the monarch might become aware of it. Having gone to the trouble of writing the book, Godwin's decision not to publish it appears to make little sense unless we accept that it was almost certainly due to his fear of the consequences had he done so. It may be that he circulated it in manuscript among trusted friends, some of whom had access to the king, but we have no evidence of this.

Taking account of the risk that his manuscript might fall into the wrong hands, Godwin, an Anglican bishop, created a main character for his book who is a Roman Catholic. The central figure in *The Man in The Moone* is Domingo Gonsales, a quixotic Spaniard with no ecclesiastical reputation to protect, in England or elsewhere.

Godwin introduces Gonsales as a man of high birth who has fallen on hard times. A military career follows. After a series of adventures in Europe, Gonsales travels to the Far East in order to escape the consequences of killing a man in a duel. Having made his fortune ('In the Indies I prospered exceedingly well') he heads back home to Spain but is taken ill as his ship rounds the Cape of Good Hope. Being close to death he is left at Saint Helena, famous at the time as a place where sailors were put ashore in the hope that they might

---

[1] In the book, necessarily for the story, this is addressed to the king of Spain but it is clearly aimed by Godwin at his own monarch.

recover from maladies such as scurvy.[2] In the event that they did, they could be picked up later when another ship called. The island had a good climate, together with fruit and fresh water, and has been described as a mid-ocean convalescent home for sailors. At this point in the story, *The Man in The Moone* is a travel narrative of its time and Godwin gives the reader a description of the island that is mostly, but not entirely, accurate.[3] He describes the 'Chappell' built by the Portuguese, the 'pretty Brooke' (today known as 'the Run') flowing past it, the 'divers faire walkes made by hand' (again, by the Portuguese), and the fruit trees, planted between these walks, 'which beare Fruit all the yeare long'.

In Godwin's time, the location and attributes of the island had already been well documented, including by his contemporary Richard Hakluyt in his *Principall Navigations* of 1589. Godwin was clearly familiar with Hakluyt's work, which includes an account of Thomas Cavendish's twelve day stay at Saint Helena in 1588, during his famous circumnavigation of the world. It is likely that Godwin had attended lectures by Hakluyt at Christ Church, Oxford: he studied there for his BA, commencing in 1578, and seems to have remained in contact afterwards with Hakluyt and his family. Hakluyt was born in Herefordshire and had both property and relatives there.

In addition, a number of other early accounts of Saint Helena were available to Godwin. It seems probable that he read the description of the island written by a Dutchman, Jan Huygen van Linschoten, who visited the island in 1589, eleven months after Cavendish. *Iohn Huighen van Linschoten his Discours of Voyages into ye Easte & West Indies* appeared in

---

[2] Hearl.
[3] Nightingales and a fox are among creatures mentioned but which are not found on Saint Helena.

print in England in 1598, complete with illustrations of the island. These images were striking, to say the least, considerably exaggerating the genuinely dramatic way that it rises so steeply from its surrounding ocean and they would have been likely to stir the imagination of anyone who came across them.

Importantly, Godwin also had access to a man who had been to Saint Helena: his near neighbour in Herefordshire, Robert Masters. It is of some interest that Masters bought his property rights at Burghill, a few miles from Hereford, from Thomas Hakluyt, a kinsman of Richard Hakluyt.

A memorial to Masters can be seen in Burghill Church. It consists of several surprisingly small brasses, although we may note that there are some of a similar size relating to other local worthies in Hereford Cathedral. Perhaps the material was an expensive commodity at the time. The brasses in Burghill Church state that Masters travelled to Virginia with 'Candish'[4] and 'afterward about the globe of ye whole worlde'. A globe is depicted on one of them. Burghill is only a mile or so from what was then the Bishop's Palace, situated in the neighbouring village of Stretton Sugwas. There are textual clues in *The Man in the Moone* that Masters and Godwin knew each other. The Virginia voyage referred to on the memorial was an entirely separate enterprise from the later circumnavigation with Cavendish. Undertaken in 1585, the Virginia voyage was in support of Raleigh's efforts to establish a colony at Roanoke, an island in what is now North Carolina. In *The Man in the Moone*, Gonsales speculates that the Lunars (the inhabitants of the Moon) and the native people of North America are related: the evidence for this being 'in regard of the continuall use of Tobacco which the Lunars use

---

[4] Thomas Cavendish.

exceeding much.' Tobacco, which occurs naturally only in North America, was then a relatively recent introduction into Europe and was popularised in England by Raleigh. Masters would have come across its use by the native population in Virginia. It is likely that he later discussed it with Godwin, causing Godwin to include a reference to it in his book.

It may have been Masters' account of Raleigh's efforts to establish a colony at Roanoke that interested Godwin in this as a potential future for Saint Helena, although no attempt to take this idea forward was made during Godwin's lifetime; the first permanent settlement was not established in Saint Helena until 1659, when it was undertaken by the East India Company under a Charter granted by Richard Protector Cromwell.

In *The Man in the Moone*, Saint Helena is uninhabited when Gonsales comes ashore there, as it would have been at the time Godwin was writing. The sole companion that Gonsales has on the island is his black servant Diego. The two of them live largely apart, purportedly to eke out the limited resources of the island[5] but actually because it is essential to the plot, as it requires means of both communication and transport to be devised between them. Prior to completing *The Man in the Moone*, Godwin had already come up with the idea of a form of telegraph, which he published somewhat sketchy details of in his *Nuncius Inanimatus* ('Lifeless Messenger') of 1629. Gonsales is described on the title page of *The Man in the Moone* as 'The Speedy Messenger' and he uses a form of signalling to keep in touch with Diego on the island. This sub-theme was clearly important to Godwin. At night, Gonsales

---

[5] Which contradicts the description given earlier by Godwin of the plentiful food made available largely through the efforts of visiting Portuguese sailors.

uses the augmented light of the Portuguese chapel tower,[6] situated in what is now Jamestown, to send messages to Diego, telling us that the walls within it were 'exceedingly white'. In daylight, Gonsales uses smoke, dust and other means that are not entirely explained to the reader, simply telling us that communication was achieved 'sometimes by a more refined and effectual way.' Godwin may well have kept the details of this to a minimum as he retained a hope that telegraphy had commercial possibilities. He had offered his proposals for this to the Crown in 1621, without success. His letter concerning this survives in The National Archives.[7]

In *The Man in the Moone*, Godwin informs us on the subject of telegraphy that '... this Art containeth more mysteries then are to be set downe in few words: Hereafter I will perhaps afford a discourse for it of purpose, assuring myself that it may prove exceedingly profitable unto mankind, being rightly used and well imployed: for that which a messenger cannot performe in many days, this may dispatch in a peece of an houre.' It is interesting to note that Saint Helena later became the place where the then most advanced visual telegraph system in the Southern Hemisphere was developed, making Godwin's description of Gonsales' efforts almost uncannily predictive. For security reasons, it was considered to be a plus point in choosing it as the place for Napoleon's imprisonment in 1815.

To transport goods and ultimately himself on Saint Helena, Gonsales invents a flying machine. The 'engine', as he calls it, is powered by birds; captured, tamed and trained by him for

---

[6] According to local legend, the Portuguese built a chapel there in 1502 from what was left of a ship considered not to be able to complete the journey back to Portugal.
[7] Ref. SP 14/120/17.

the purpose. These are a type of wild swan[8], actually unknown then or now on the island, which he terms 'gansas'. From Gonsales' description of his maiden flight,[9] we know that it was across what is now James Bay, from Munden's Point to West Rocks. We can work this out from the fact that he set off from near the stream, now known as the Run, that emerged then on the opposite side of the bay from where it enters the sea today, through a culvert. There is both science and sense in Gonsales' first flight being over water – it is safer. When Neil Armstrong, Edwin 'Buzz' Aldrin and Michael Collins returned from the Moon in 1969 they splashed down in the sea. In Gonsales' case it was a precaution against him not making it to West Rocks: 'the worse that could be, was but to fall into the water, where being able to swim well, I hoped to receive little or no hurt in my fall.'

Elated by his success in becoming 'the first flying man', Gonsales resolves to take his invention back to Spain with him as soon as the opportunity might arise, which it does in the form of a visiting fleet on its way back from the East Indies. He succeeds in gaining passages for himself and Diego, together with the gansas and his 'engine', but when his ship reaches Tenerife it is pursued by English pirates.

Gonsales escapes by using his flying machine and then finds himself on 'El Pico'. Here, we again have Godwin using contemporary travel narratives: Hakluyt had included an account by an Englishman, Thomas Nicols, in his *Principall Navigations*, suggesting that El Pico, known today as Pico del Teide, is 15 leagues (45 miles) in height, and Godwin repeats this. In fact, it rises to 12,198 feet, significantly less than a league, although this still makes it the highest point above sea level in the Atlantic islands. On the slopes of El Pico, Gonsales

---

[8] Sometimes referred to as geese in later works.
[9] He had previously put a sheep aloft.

is threatened by hostile natives and is forced to take off again, with the astonishing consequence that he is carried to the Moon. This is where the science comes in, not through his fanciful means of transport but in what he experiences both during the 'voyage thither' and following his arrival at his unintended destination.

Gonsales reports a sensation of weightlessness during his journey and that the gansas proceed apparently effortlessly but at greater speed once free from the pull of the Earth. This is fairly advanced stuff: Isaac Newton, who first formulated the theory of gravity, had yet to be born. But Godwin puts this down to magnetic force, 'the attractive Beams of that tyrannous Loadstone the earth.' He appears to have been influenced in this by William Gilbert's *De Magnete*, published in 1600.

During his flight, Gonsales is able to confirm the theory of Copernicus, which was increasingly gaining acceptance at the time, that the Earth rotates: '...all the Countries of our earthly world within the compasse of 24 howers were represented to my sight.' Interestingly, Robert Hues, another Herefordshire man who had sailed with Cavendish, was also a champion of Copernican theory. Hues may have visited Saint Helena with Cavendish in 1588, certainly he was with him during the 1591/1592 voyage, which approached Saint Helena but failed to effect a landing there. Hues is famous for his *Tractatus de globis et eorum usu* ('Treatise on Globes and Their Use') published in 1594, in which he makes four references to Saint Helena and supports the idea that the Earth is a sphere.

Once on the lunar surface Gonsales discovers that it is capable of supporting life and that there are humans there. As befits a character created by a bishop, Gonsales first tests the religious credentials of its inhabitants: 'I crossed myself, and cried out, *Iesus Maria.*' Following this, the 'Lunars' all immediately fall to their knees, convincing Gonsales of their faith. This issue out of the way, we learn more about the locals, including that they live long lives, unaffected by such nuisances as crime – a state of perfection ensured by consigning troublesome children to Earth. Godwin was clearly familiar with the story of the 'green children' who were said to have turned up in Suffolk in the twelfth century.[10] Perhaps it was this story that first gave us green as the much favoured colour for extra-terrestrials. The tale of the green children makes mention of Saint Martin and it is interesting to note that in Gonsales' account of the Lunars' beliefs he runs through the names of the saints until he gets to '*St. Martinus*', at which point the Lunars hold up their hands 'in signe of great reverence'. We are then told that '*Martin* in their language signifieth God.'

Gonsales goes on to find that both trees and people are taller on the Moon than they are on Earth. He tells us that the trees grow '30 times more than ours' and that our lunar cousins are 'for the most part' twice the height of ourselves. The reported height of the Lunars owes at least something to travel narratives of the time, in which there are stories of giants in the then newly discovered world: notably in what we now know as Patagonia. Antonio Pigafetta, in his account of the first circumnavigation of the globe, which is generally known as Magellan's, although he did not survive the enterprise, told of a man who was of such stature that: '… the tallest of us only came up to his waist.' But, in *The Man in the Moone*, Godwin is making a scientific point. There may not be giants in Patagonia, but what of humans on the Moon once they are

---

[10] William of Newburgh, *On the Green Children*, (1196-98); see Appendix C in Poole.

subject to a lesser force of what we now know as gravity?[11] They would be taller, as the trees would be as well. Cultivation of trees has yet to be undertaken at the International Space Station, but we do know, from data recorded on board, that astronauts grow taller in space: up to two inches in the case of one who is already a six-footer. But reduced gravity simply stretches the spine and the additional height is not retained on return to Earth.[12] That said, Godwin's point is clear, people and plants might well be taller on the Moon than they are on Earth.

As Gonsales explores the Moon he experiences much that is worthy of including in his subsequent memoir. Some of this is merely fanciful but aspects of it, as with the idea that plants and people might grow taller on the Moon, do explore elements of science. We have for example the way the Lunars move around the Moon. As Godwin describes it:

> 'I must let you understand that the *Globe* of the *Moone* is not altogether destitute of an attractive Power: but it is so farre weaker than that of the earth, as if a man doe but spring upward, with all his force, ... he shall be able to mount 50. or 60 foote high...'

It is tempting to think that Godwin might well have felt vindicated had he lived to see the footage of men actually walking on the surface of the Moon, struggling, as they did, to maintain contact with it even when suitably weighed down by their space suits.

---

[11] A term not used by Godwin.

[12] In 2018, Japanese Astronaut, Norishige Kanai, claimed that he had gained three-and-a-half inches during his first three weeks at the International Space Station. He was forced to apologise – for extending the truth rather more than he had his spine. The Russian commander doubted his claim and the true height gain was found to be three-quarters of an inch. *Daily Mail*, 11 January 2018, p.32.

Godwin also raises the possibility that colours may be different on the Moon: he reports a colour that is 'never seen in our earthly world'. It follows from this that it is impossible for him to describe it in terms of the colours we all see on Earth, but Gonsales tells us that of all his lunar experiences this was the one that most 'delighted' him. In fact, as we now know, the Moon is somewhat lacking in colour. Frank Borman, Commander of the first manned flight around the Moon, said in a radio interview to mark his 90th birthday that there was '…no colour at all. Just different shades of grey'.[13]

When Gonsales returns to Earth the time taken is only eight days, compared to the twelve days of his moonward flight. A modern mathematician, Andrew J Simoson, has shown that this demonstrates a considerable mathematical ability on the part of Godwin. The longer time taken for the outward journey is explained by what is termed a 'pursuit curve' – a spacecraft heading for the Moon is pursuing a moving object and does not head in a straight line. The return trip is somewhat different. In 1968, Apollo 8, the mission commanded by Frank Borman, took 3.5 days to get to the Moon, but returned to Earth in only 2.5 days.

Apollo 8 came down in the sea, as Gonsales did in his maiden flight across James Bay. In *The Man in the Moone* Gonsales does not splash down on his return, finding himself in China, where he is initially treated as a threat and imprisoned. His difficulties there are eventually overcome and he is then able to send the manuscript account of his adventures back to Europe through the agency of some Jesuit missionaries from Spain. These are traceable to China at that time and their names can be shown to be those used by Godwin. It is almost certain that these missionaries returned to

---

[13] *Daily Mail*, 1 September 2018.

Europe via Saint Helena (it would have been the conventional route) although we have no record of this. It is interesting to note that some Christian converts from Japan visited the island in 1588, having been captured and brought there by Cavendish during his circumnavigation, which may have prompted Godwin to come up with the idea of how a manuscript might be brought back from the Orient. Robert Masters of Burghill, the near neighbour of Francis Godwin, was among their travelling companions.

II
Godwin's Legacy

We do not know whose decision it was to submit *The Man in the Moone* for publication. The manuscript may have been left by Godwin with directions that it should be published after his death; more likely, it was simply found among his papers and considered by a family member to be marketable. Godwin may not even have given it the title by which we now know it. There was a vogue at the time for books speculating about life on the Moon; including Johannes Kepler's *Somnium* ('The Dream'), published in 1634, and Wilkins' *The Discovery of a World in the Moone*, which appeared in 1638. What we do know is that Godwin's son Paul was apprenticed to John Bill, who had printed previous works by Godwin and that Paul finished his apprenticeship in 1635. Another former apprentice of John Bill's was Joshua Kirton and it was Kirton and a Thomas Warren who gained and registered a licence for the publication of *The Man in the Moone* in 1638. Godwin's authorship was not acknowledged in the first edition. Instead, the book was said to have been 'written in Spanish by DOMINGO GONSALES and translated into English by EDWARD MAHON gent.' Edward Mahon has not been identified and is probably an invented character. The book, written in English by Godwin, clearly did not need a translator.

The famous engraving of Gonsales aloft in his flying machine, with El Pico in the background, must have been commissioned in preparation for the book going to print: if Godwin had seen it he would have pointed out that the number of gansas depicted is in conflict with what he had written; the text requires there to be twenty-five, but the engraving shows only ten.

The Man in the Moone had something for just about everybody, appealing to a wide range of readers. History is in it at the outset, with the book's setting being in the sixteenth rather than the seventeenth century in which it was written. It commences with the birth of Gonsales in Seville in 1552 and traces his military career during the conflict in what was then the Spanish Netherlands, where the protestant Dutch were fighting against the Spanish forces led by Duke Fernando Alvarez de Toledo, the third Duke of Alva. We then have a travel narrative, popular at the time, in which Gonsales visits the East Indies, China, Saint Helena and Tenerife. Readers also noted the picaresque element in the book and saw Gonsales as a Don Quixote type figure. Lady Brilliana Harley, one of the earliest readers of the book, saw in it 'some kine to Donqueshot'.[1] The English have always had some difficulty with the pronunciation of Don Quixote.

The book was an immediate success, a best seller as we would term it today, and it remained popular for a long time afterwards, being translated from its original English into French, Dutch, German, and, it seems, Italian, although no copy of an Italian version survives. *The Man in the Moone* ran to at least twenty-four editions.

---

[1] Cited by Poole, p.47.

It is interesting to note that one of the earliest readers of *The Man in the Moone* was a Dutchman, Michael Florent van Langren ('Langrenus'), a noted astronomer and cartographer, who in 1645 produced a map of the moon showing a crater that he named 'Gansii'. Poole notes that this is 'the only fictional referent in his selenography [a description of the Moon's surface]'.[2] The crater is now named 'Halley', after Edmond Halley, who we will return to later.

The Man in the Moone has been plagiarised, satirised and, in some of its religious content, bowdlerised; its various editions contain both omissions and additions: taking account of what was regarded as of continuing interest (or not) and what it was politic to print at the time. It influenced a considerable number of writers up to and including the present day. We will look at some of these now.

Cyrano de Bergerac is best remembered today for his large nose and great skill as a swordsman, but he was also a writer. Much of what we believe ourselves to know about him is based on a play, *Cyrano de Bergerac*, by the French poet Edmond Rostand, published in 1897. This led to an early film of the same name, released in 1900, starring Benoit-Constant Cocqueli. A significant number of films based on much the same story have appeared subsequently, with at least nine bearing exactly the same title: including those starring Christopher Plummer in 1962, Derek Jacobi in 1985, Gerard Depardieu in 1990 and Kevin Kline in 2008. But the film treatment has tended to divert attention from de Bergerac's achievements as an author. In his day, and for some years after his death, Cyrano de Bergerac was a much read writer, an exponent during the first half of the seventeenth century of what became known as libertine literature. Centred mostly on

---

[2] See Poole, p. 49, citing Ewen A. Whitaker, *Mapping and Naming the Moon: A History of Lunar Cartography and Nomenclarure*, p. 41.

contemporary France, writers in this style attempted to cast off the conventional moral and sexual restraints of the time. Against this background it is unsurprising that in his treatment of *The Man in the Moone* Cyrano de Bergerac decided on satire. The narrator in his *Comical History of the States and Empires of the Worlds of the Moon*, published posthumously in 1657, is Cyrano himself, or at least shares his name. The Cyrano of the book has a wish to fly to the Moon. He first attempts this by strapping bottles of dew to his body, which, unsurprisingly, is unsuccessful. He next uses a flying machine, in which he crashes as he tries to get airborne by jumping off a cliff. Soldiers then attach rockets to what remains of it as part of the celebrations marking the feast day of St. John the Baptist. Trapped on board as he tries to save his machine Cyrano is carried into space and lands on the Moon. This seems to be the earliest example of rocket powered exploration of space. To this extent, Cyrano de Bergerac follows Godwin's idea of an accidental astronaut, another theme that we will come back to later. Cyrano the spaceman finds that the Gonsales of *The Man in the Moone* is still in residence there; where because of his Spanish clothing and his diminutive stature he has been taken for an ape. According to Cyrano, it was the custom of the Lunars to dress their apes in Spanish style. No doubt this was considered humorous at the time. Cyrano engages Gonsales in a series of heretical discussions, perhaps a jibe at Godwin. There is plenty of science, fictional and otherwise, in the *Comical History*: including the rocket powered flight and speculation that the sun will one day run out of fuel, but before that occurs, the harnessing of solar energy.

In *The Emperor of the Moon*, written in 1688, Aphra Behn went for comic drama. Behn was one of the foremost playwrights of the period and is believed to have been the first

Englishwoman to have earned a living from her writing. Her own story is the stuff that films are made of, although it is often difficult to unravel fact from fiction in the details of her life. If the seemingly eye witness accounts in her novel *Oroonoko* are genuinely autobiographical, she travelled to South America at the age of twenty-three, to what is now Suriname, perhaps venturing further up the Orinoco river than any European before her. Certainly, she was a spy. She operated in Antwerp during the Second Anglo-Dutch War under the code name 'Agent 160'. In the Prologue to her play *Forc'd Marriage* she wrote: 'The Poetess too, they say, has Spies abroad.' Behn was clearly an avid reader as well as writer and knew the literary tastes of the period. An audience's familiarity with *The Man in the Moone* is assumed by her in *The Emperor of the Moon* and is mentioned early in the play, the structure of which is that of the Italian *commedia dell'arte*. Various of the stock characters from that form appear in the play, including Scaramouch and Harlequin. Central to the plot is that a Doctor Baliardo[3] has done a great deal of reading of scientific works, 'foolish books' as his daughter Elaria puts it, which have had the effect of turning his mind. His particular taste is for works based on astronomy, including 'an heroic business called *The Man in the Moon*, if you'll believe a Spaniard, who was carried thither, upon an engine drawn by wild geese;...'. It becomes clear that Baliardo is convinced that the Moon is inhabited by beings superior to those on Earth, with the result that only potential husbands from there will make acceptable suitors for Elaria and his niece Bellemante. But the girls are already in love. With the complicity of Scaramouch, a servant of Baliardo, they have been meeting the characters Don Cinthio and Don Charmante in secret. To solve the problem posed by

---

[3] 'Balardo' in the *commedia dell'arte*.

Baliardo's likely rejection of these matches, a plot is hatched to pass off Don Cinthio and Don Charmante as visitors from the Moon, who appear respectively in the play as the 'Prince of Thunderland' and the 'Emperor'. The action becomes a farce within a farce, with the unwitting Baliardo being the only character who is unaware that what is being acted out before him is an elaborate trick intended to enable the two girls to marry their lovers. In order for this to be achieved Baliardo's interest in astronomy must be harnessed. Act 1, Scene 2, commences with the stage direction:

> *'Enter Doctor, with all manner of mathematical instruments hanging at his girdle; Scaramouch bearing a telescope twenty (or more) foot long.'*

The telescope is an essential prop. Baliardo is told that an important visitor has arrived to see him: Don Charmante, masquerading as an emissary from *The Emperor of the Moon*. Don Charmante invites Baliardo to look through the telescope, placing over the end of it 'a glass with a picture of a nymph', followed by another which appears to show the emperor. Baliardo is easily convinced that he has viewed both a lunar nymph, Egeria, and 'the mighty Iredonozar': the name of the latter being derived from Godwin's Irdonozur, 'the great Monarch' of *The Man in the Moone*. There is also mention of 'a certain stone they call the Ebula.' In *The Man in the Moone*, the 'Ebulus' is a stone given to Gonsales by Irdonozur which has the power of being able to control the weight of anyone who uses it, with one side 'clapt to the bare skin of a man' reducing it and the other side similarly applied increasing it. When Gonsales returns to Earth he is able to slow his descent by using the stone, thus ensuring a safe landing.

In due course, Don Cinthio and Don Charmante, having passed themselves off as being from the Moon, are able to secure Baliardo's approval for them to marry Elaria and Bellemante. The play ends with the plot being revealed to a much chastened Baliardo. Johannes Kepler and Galileo then appear as characters. Galileo says little and is presumably simply included as the populariser of the telescope, a version of which has featured so prominently in the play. It is left to Kepler, who had speculated in his *Somnium* of 1634 that the Moon might be inhabited, to bring Baliardo out of his madness. Baliardo recognises that he has been a fool and declares: 'Burn all my books, and let my study blaze; …I see there's nothing in philosophy.' Although a borrowing from *Doctor Faustus* ('I'll burn my books') would seem to be evident here, Marlowe's plays were not in fashion in the late seventeenth century and Behn would not have been able to assume any familiarity with them on the part of her audience. Bearing in mind the frequency of comparisons at the time between *The Man in the Moone* and *Don Quixote* it is more likely that Behn had in mind Don Quixote's rejection of his books when he finds that they have deceived him. Certainly, Don Quixote gains a mention early in the play, when Scaramouch addresses Elaria with the lines, 'You must know, madam, your father, (my master the doctor) is a little whimsical, romantic, or Don Quick-sottish, or so.'

The Emperor of the Moon is comical, clever and still regularly performed; and it tells us a great deal about the knowledge of science, both real and fictional, that its original audience was assumed to have when it attended a performance. 'Gravity' appears twice in the script, arguably as a pun, and it presented an opportunity for extemporisation by the actors, an important element of the *commedia dell'arte* tradition. Newton's theory of gravity had been presented to the

Royal Society in 1686 and his *Principia*,[4] containing it, was published a year later: it was, therefore, a topical subject when Behn's play appeared.

The Man in the Moone also became part of the popular travel literature of the period. *A View of the English Acquisitions in Guinea and the East Indies*, by 'R.B.', appeared in 1686 and it promised its readers:

> 'An Account of the Religion, Government, Wars, Strange Customs, Beasts, Serpents, Monsters and other Observables in those Countries. Together with A Description of the Isle of St. Helena;...'

The 'R.B.' stood for Richard Burton, a pseudonym of Nathaniel Crouch, a London printer and bookseller. He was more of a compiler than an original author and some have considered him a systematic plagiariser of the works of others. As his contemporary, John Dunton, politely put it, '... his talent lies at collection': but Crouch produced a huge number of popular and affordable books, mostly on historical themes. *A View of the English Acquisitions in Guinea and the East Indies*, as its title suggests, commences with a treatment of Guinea and ends with an account, which is somewhat lacking in detail, of the East Indies. Between Guinea and the East Indies, both geographically and in Crouch's work, are Saint Helena and Saldana Bay, the latter being in what is now South Africa. In dealing with Saint Helena, Crouch prints a version of *The Man in the Moone*, adapted by himself, which takes up a major part of the book. He acknowledges Godwin's original authorship: but only to the extent that it was written by 'a learned Bishop'. Almost certainly, he took this from what John Wilkins had written almost half a century earlier: 'I chanced

---

[4] *Philosophiae Naturalis Principia Mathematica.*

upon a late fancy to this purpose under the fained name of Domingo Gonsales, written by a late reverend and learned Bishop.' Crouch's stated reason for padding out a book intended to provide an informative overview of foreign places with a work of fiction was, he suggested, to prevent the work from fading into obscurity. The effect of this was to preserve *The Man in the Moone* in a form that differs from the one first published and which much influenced the content of later editions. Importantly, it firmly placed the book back in its Saint Helena context, where it was to remain. Saint Helena was a big selling point and Crouch took full advantage of this, writing:

'Before I come to relate the acquisitions of the English in India, etc., I will make a halt at St. Hellens, or Helena; which is now possessed by the hon. East India Company, It is called the Sea-inn, because the English, and other nations stop there, as a place for watering and refreshment, in their long voyages to India.'

The image of Saint Helena became that of an inn of the ocean: an important place, providing as it did the water and food essential for voyages to and from India.

The title page of the 1768 edition of *The Man in the Moone*, eighty years later, shows clearly that the book's connection with Saint Helena remained a significant factor as far as sales were concerned, stating that it contained:

'An account of the Island of St. HELLENA; the Place where He [Gonsales] resided some Years in, and where he planned this Wonderful Voyage;...'

This was, of course, inaccurate in two regards: Gonsales' sojourn on Saint Helena was only a little over a year, and his trip to the Moon ('this Wonderful Voyage') was an unplanned one. But it left Saint Helena centre stage.

III
A Hollow Earth

Edmond Halley, an early visitor to Saint Helena, is best known today for having predicted the re-appearance of the comet that now bears his name, an event which he calculated occurs around every 76 years. It is Halley who worked out that it orbits the sun as the planets do. It had been recorded at various times in the past, including shortly before the Norman invasion of England in 1066 (it is depicted in the Bayeux Tapestry), but Halley recognised that it was a recurring astronomical event and not simply a series of unconnected arrivals of various objects that could be seen from Earth. In his *Synopsis of the Astronomy of Planets*, published in 1705, he suggested that the comet, which he had seen himself in 1682, would again be visible from Earth in 'about' 1758: and he was right – it was next spotted by Johann Georg Palitzsch, a German farmer and amateur astronomer, on 25 December of that year. Unfortunately, Halley did not live to enjoy this moment of success, he died in 1742; but his achievement brought him considerable posthumous fame. As he had also predicted.

Born in London in 1656, Halley attended Saint Paul's School in London and then moved on to Queen's College, Oxford, in 1673, which he left without taking a degree. At Oxford he had become interested in the work of John

Flamsteed, the first Astronomer Royal, a position that had been established by Charles II as recently as 1667. Flamsteed set himself the task of compiling a full record of the northern stars, the ones visible from the Northern Hemisphere. Halley, who was destined to become the second Astronomer Royal, planned to do the same for the stars that may be seen principally from the Southern Hemisphere. His observatory for this would be on Saint Helena.

The essentials of Halley's project were relatively easy for him to achieve; he had both a wealthy father and a near neighbour who owned a ship that served the island. He also had support in the form of Robert Boyle, of Boyle's Law fame, who happened to be a director of the East India Company, which then governed Saint Helena under a charter granted by the Crown.[1] The final requirement, although the project seems to have been largely put together by this time anyway, was a letter of instruction, politely couched as a recommendation, from King Charles II to the East India Company. This requested that Halley and a friend, who is unnamed in the letter, be given a free passage to Saint Helena, where 'they are desirous to go & remain for some time to make observations of the planets & stars, for rectifying and finishing the celestial globe.'[2] The grant of this royal favour was considerably influenced by the lack of any cost to the king: the passage to the island would be the responsibility of the East India Company and, while there, Halley would receive £300 a year, a significant sum at the time, from his father, a London soap merchant, who also equipped him with instruments which were considerably more expensive and of greater accuracy than those then available to Flamsteed at Greenwich.

---

[1] This had superseded the one granted by Richard Protector Cromwell in 1659.

[2] I have modernised the spelling.

Halley made the most of the three month voyage to the island, particularly in regard to the finer points of navigation: he was later to become the captain of a ship in his own right. He used the time and his experience on board to give consideration to the question of magnetic variation, sometimes referred to as 'declination', which had proved to be something of a problem for seafarers. As is well known, magnetic north is not the same as geographical or 'true' north, the North Pole above which hovers the North Star. A compass needle points towards magnetic north. Early charts allowed for this in their depiction of what are termed rhumb lines. A rhumb line is the line theoretically taken by a vessel sailing on a constant compass bearing. These appeared on charts as webs of lines oriented from compass rose points, which allowed for adjustment to take account of the difference between magnetic north and true north. These were accurate enough for the needs of sailors operating over relatively short routes, but not for oceanic navigation. Magnetic variation is the difference between magnetic and true north, but it carries with it the problem that the angle showing this difference varies according to the position on the earth's surface of a person attempting to navigate in reliance upon it, rendering rhumb lines inadequate for their intended purpose during long voyages. Magnetic north also has the unfortunate characteristic of altering its position on the earth's surface over relatively short periods of time. As I write, magnetic north is proceeding away from its historic home in Canada towards Siberia at a rate of around 25 miles a year.

We may reasonably assume that Halley, in his consideration of the question of magnetic variation, had already dismissed the traditional idea that it was caused by sailors chewing onions and garlic during their voyages. This had originated with Pliny the Elder in Roman times and seems to have persisted until Giambattista della Porta revealed in his *Magiae Naturalis* of 1558 that sailors regarded it as no more than a fable and that they would 'sooner lose their lives than abstain from eating onyons and garlick.'

Halley did, however, give serious thought to a theory that magnetic variation was caused by a gradual build-up and shifting of iron ore deposits. He concluded fairly quickly during the voyage that it had nothing to do with the movement of these either: he needed to come up with something better. Much of the data on which he later relied when formulating his own theory was gathered while at sea and collated during his time on Saint Helena.[3]

Halley and his friend, a Mr Clerke, arrived at Saint Helena in February 1677 to find that life on the island was far from comfortable, even precarious. The East India Company's right to be there had been challenged by a Dutch invasion and brief occupation as recently as 1672-73. Against this background, accommodating a twenty-year old astronomer was unlikely to have been something the then governor, Gregory Field, would have treated as a priority.

Halley chose a site for his observatory that has since been re-invented as a covered picnic spot. The shelter now provided for picnickers offers a clear clue that the site might be less than suitable for purposes of astronomy. Situated near Hutt's Gate, on high ground, it is one of the wettest places on the island. There were, however, other scientific issues that could be pondered during a damp and cloudy night at Hutt's Gate. We do not know how far his thoughts on magnetic variation progressed while he was enduring frustrating nights at his observatory, only that he had already gathered much of the

[3] See N. Kollerstrom, *The Hollow World of Edmond Halley, Jnl. for History of Astronomy*, 1992, 23, 185-192.

material that he eventually used in formulating his idea for explaining it. His conclusion was that the Earth is hollow.

He was to work on this theory for the next thirteen years, presenting it to the Royal Society in 1691.[4] The world as he saw it was comparable to a Russian doll, although he did not use this metaphor – these had yet to be invented. It consisted, he suggested, of a number of globes within globes, all of which are encased in the outer one which we recognise as Earth. In his model, there were four magnetic poles, two on a fixed outer sphere and two on a westward rotating inner one, a conclusion that he had reached as early as 1683. Importantly, as the idea has lived on in science fiction, he suggested that the interior of the Earth was capable of supporting life – 'I have adventured to make these subterranean orbs capable of being inhabited.' The inner world was, he speculated, illuminated, and 'may in several places shine with such a substance as invests the surface of the Sun.'[5]

The presentation date of his paper to the Royal Society towards the end of 1691, in November of that year, is of some significance. As we have seen, he was under suspicion of atheism at the time, which is what brought about his failure to gain appointment as Savilian Professor of Astronomy at Oxford; his rival for the post, David Gregory, was elected in preference to Halley in December 1691. With this in mind, we should not be surprised that Halley's paper dealt with religious as well as scientific issues. A part of his theory relied on an acceptance that our world is not destined to last for ever, which

---

[4] E. Halley, 'An account of the cause of the change of the variation of the magnetic needle with an hypothesis of the structure of the inner parts of the Earth', published in *Philosophical Transactions,* xvi (1692), 653-87.

[5] When called upon by the Royal Society to explain the appearance of an aurora borealis in March 1716, which was clearly visible from England, even in daytime, he attributed it to luminous material emerging from inside the Earth through fissures at the North Pole.

is in accordance with what the Bible teaches us, including in Revelation 21: 'And I saw a new heaven and a new earth: for the first heaven and the first earth were passed away; and there was no more sea.'[6] Atheism was associated with a belief that Earth is eternal, it having been shown by geologists to have been around for a great deal longer than a literal reading of the Bible indicates. As far as atheists were concerned, Earth was destined to remain in existence indefinitely. Halley was at pains to point out that his idea of an inhabited inner Earth accorded with 'Almighty Wisdom', his argument being that God would not have so arranged things in a way 'barely to support' life by restricting it to the Earth's surface. What had been created by the Almighty must be considered in its entirety, including whatever lies below the terrestrial world as we know it. In terms of Christian orthodoxy this seems to have been regarded by some as a reasonable theological argument. Writing in reference to Halley's theory in 1717, William Whiston, a writer on both religious matters and astronomy, came up with scriptural support for it in his *Astronomical Principles of Religion*.[7]

It seems that the idea of an inner world was one of the things that Halley hoped to be remembered for: in the last of the seventeen known portraits of him, painted when he was eighty years of age, he is shown holding a picture of a hollow Earth. The idea did not survive later scientific scrutiny and it proved to be the theory itself that was hollow. Nevertheless, and however scientifically unsound, the endorsement of the idea of an inhabited underworld, put forward by a serious scientist of some stature, gave credibility to ancient myths. It also seemed to support the underlying premise of at least one then recent work of science fiction, Margaret Cavendish's *The*

---

[6] King James Bible (1611).
[7] Kollerstrom, p.189, and endnote 38.

Blazing World, which was published in 1666. Somewhat unfortunately for the choice of its title this was also the year of the Great Fire of London. In Cavendish's work, the interior of the Earth is reached via the North Pole: the heroine finds talking animals in the inner world, becomes empress there and subsequently launches an invasion of the outer world using submarines. Cavendish, along with Aphra Behn, is deserving of a place in feminist history.

Once Halley had given Cavendish's idea some scientific credence it was taken up by a number of other writers of science fiction, including in *Niels Klim's Underground Travels*, by Ludvig Holberg, published in 1741.[8] In Holberg's work, the fictional Klim has studied philosophy and theology at the University of Copenhagen. Returning to his native Bergen, in Norway, he comes across a cave above the town which provides him with an opening into the inner earth, where he finds that there is a planet, which he calls Nazar, orbiting around a subterranean sun. The inhabitants of Nazar are monkeys.

Similar books were soon produced in England, including *A Voyage to the World in the Centre of the Earth*, which was published anonymously in London in 1755. The author has remained unidentified. The narrator of the story exhausts his meagre inheritance as a younger son, gains employment on a ship, and travels to Italy, where he falls through a succession of apparently endless holes while visiting Mount Vesuvius. Plummeting to a seemingly certain death his life is saved when he lands on a conveniently positioned haystack, where he finds himself stuck because of the increased gravitational pull brought about by the depth to which he has fallen.[9]

---

[8] In Latin, *Nicolai Klimii Iter Subterraneum*.

[9] In fact, he would have experienced the opposite of this. Gravitational pull decreases towards the centre of the earth.

Fortunately, a sympathetic intra-terrestrial soon arrives on the scene and applies a salve, which enables our hero to get up. Further treatment also renders him capable of conversing in the local language, which serves to help the story along. The tale largely takes the form of a travel narrative, a popular subject at the time. It promises: 'an Account of the Manners, Customs, Laws, Government and Religion of the Inhabitants.' There is even mention of colonialism, then still in its infancy. It seems that problems have been caused by the arrival in the inner world of English settlers: the result being that the local king has adopted a policy of restricting all terrestrials who subsequently arrive there to a stay of one year, an early example of formulating an immigration policy. We also learn that the indigenous inhabitants are vegetarians, who live for two hundred years or more and rely on giant birds for transport, perhaps reflecting the lingering influence of *The Man in the Moone* and Godwin's gansas. When the narrator returns to the surface of the Earth he arrives at a spot within easy reach of London at a location which he agrees not to reveal. He is soon able to indulge in the things that he has been missing, such as boiled artichokes, cream cheese and salad.

Most famously in the canon of science fiction, the idea of the globe being hollow continued with *A Journey to the Centre of the Earth* by Jules Verne in 1864.[10] In this, the characters travel to Snaefell, a dormant volcano in Iceland. Descending into its crater, they find a subterranean ocean. Following a series of adventures featuring what to us is prehistoric life – including mastodons, the North American relatives of mammoths – they eventually surface via the crater of Stromboli, in southern Italy. Again, we have the influence of earlier works, such as *A Voyage to the World in the Centre of*

---

[10] Originally published in French.

the Earth, with volcanoes being the key to entering the inner world.

The question of intra-terrestrial life has never gone completely away, either in science or science fiction. We will come across it again later when looking at Thomas Pynchon's *Mason & Dixon*, a significant part of which is set on Saint Helena.

Interestingly, modern scientists have shown that life forms do exist at a far greater depth within the Earth than was previously thought possible and there is a growing body of support for the idea that life on the surface of the Earth may have evolved from primitive organisms within it. Similarly, life elsewhere in the Universe, perhaps on Mars, may simply be hidden from us for now by it being sub-surface. The claim that an underground lake has been identified on Mars made headlines in 2018, including the suggestion that it has the potential for offering the conditions necessary for life.

IV
A Visit to the Lunar Sphere

A Visit to the Lunar Sphere, a short story that appeared in *Blackwood's Edinburgh Magazine* in November 1820, shows that *The Man in the Moone* continued to influence writers almost two hundred years after it was first published: and that new works could still be written based on the assumption that a reader would be familiar with Godwin's book. But technology had moved on. With the arrival on the scene of a convincing alternative to bird-power the story could be progressed, if only in fun. *A Visit to the Lunar Sphere* is intended to be humorous rather than seriously scientific. By the time it was written, a number of men, and at least one woman, had actually flown, and the word 'aeronaut' had entered the English language.

The use of balloons as a means of flight was pioneered in France, commencing in 1783, just six years before the revolution. Two brothers, Joseph and Etienne Montgolfier, were pivotal in this, using hot air balloons as a way of publicising the products of their paper mill – the idea is said to have come from them seeing a paper bag, one of their own of course, floating away when used to cover a pot of boiling coffee. A ten metre wide version of the 'cloud in a paper bag', powered by a brazier, was demonstrated in Paris on 19 September 1783, but with the underlying science of the idea not yet fully understood the Montgolfiers thought it to be smoke that did the trick. With this in mind, damp straw, decomposed meat and old shoes were used as fuel. Louis XVI and Marie Antoinette, who attended the event, were unimpressed, perhaps because of the stench, and quickly quit the scene. Although royal approval was not immediate the idea soon took hold, albeit with some adjustment of the fuel mix. Versailles was treated later that year to the sight of a sheep, cockerel and a duck being lifted into the air. There seems to have been an element of prescience in Godwin having selected a sheep as the animal first sent aloft by Gonsales at Saint Helena.

The next step, as with Gonsales and his 'engine', had to be a manned flight, using hot air as the updated means of getting aloft. Condemned prisoners were considered for both the honour and the risk of being the first men to fly, and Louis XVI was happy to provide some: but in the event it fell to two free men, Jean-Francois Pilâtre de Rozier and the Marquis d'Arlandes. Following some preliminary tests using balloons tethered to the ground by ropes, they set off from the Bois de Boulogne in Paris on 21 November 1783 and landed around thirty minutes later at Butte-aux-Cailles, some ten kilometres south-east of their casting off point. By December of the same year, Jacques Alexander César Charles and Nicolas-Louise Robert had extended the range of a balloon to thirty-five kilometres, touching down in the village of Nesles-la-Vallée.

Charles, a physicist, had by then introduced hydrogen for extra lift, contained in what is known in ballooning circles as an 'envelope'. Along the way, the aeronauts rose to a height of around five hundred and fifty metres. Inspired by their success, Charles insisted on going up again the same day. He achieved a height of three thousand metres, experiencing severe ear-ache in the process due to the sharp fall in pressure. To this day, hydrogen balloons are called Charlières in France.[1]

As is so often the case once there has been an important new scientific discovery or technological advance, further progress came quickly. The 1785 Rozier balloon made use of helium to supplement hot air. In 1804, Louis Joseph Gay-Lussac, another physicist, achieved a record ascent of seven thousand metres – over four miles.

It is interesting that the first recorded instance of aerial combat occurred only four years later, when two Frenchmen, a Monsieur de Grandpré and a Monsieur le Pique fought a duel with blunderbusses from two balloons floating above Paris, the issue at stake being the affections of a certain Mademoiselle Tirevit. It seems unlikely that either of the men expected to die: they had agreed only to shoot so as to deflate the balloon, pride and amorous ambition of the other; but Le Pique's balloon collapsed more quickly than expected when hit and he and his second plunged to their deaths.

The British scientific establishment remained strangely unmoved by what they saw as little more than a form of popular entertainment: and popular it was, the Paris flight by Charles and Robert had attracted a crowd of several hundred thousand, around half the population of Paris at the time. The

---

[1] Steve Jones, *No Need for Geniuses*, p.189. A hot air balloon is a *Montgolfière*: see *The Man With His Head in the Clouds*, Richard O. Smith, p.35.

duel of 1808 was observed by a more modest number. Perhaps the lesser turnout on this occasion was because of the uncongenial dawn start and that its true purpose, which might have drawn a larger number of spectators, had not been publicised, it being billed simply as a balloon race. Duelling was illegal in France at the time.

The first manned flight in England, on 15 September 1784, was by Vincenzo Lunardi, an Italian, whose balloon ascended from Moorfields in London and carried him to Standon Green End in Hertfordshire. There had been a short stopover at Welham Green on the way to release an accompanying cat that was suffering from airsickness, perhaps the first recorded case of this condition. A plaque at the final landing site suggests that Lunardi's achievement was due to 'the power of chemistry and the fortitude of man': assisted, it is respectfully added, by the watchful eye of the Almighty. Lunardi, whose name seems particularly apt for an aeronaut, gained some fame but did not move the technology much forward. This was left to James Sadler of Oxford.

Sadler, who is not much remembered today, was the first Englishman to fly. He ascended in a 'fire balloon'[2] from Christ Church Meadow, Oxford, on 4 October 1784, reaching around 3,600 feet, and landed shortly afterwards at Wood Eaton, some six miles to the north of Oxford. According to Sadler's biographer, Richard O. Smith, Sadler almost certainly intended this to be a largely unwitnessed event: in case it went wrong. Almost inevitably, the press got wind of it, turned up to cover the story and an item about it quickly followed in *Jackson's Oxford Journal*, 'in quite astounding detail'.[3] By 12 November Sadler had progressed to a hydrogen filled balloon,

[2] The description of it given on a plaque in nearby Deadman's Walk.
[3] Smith, p.14.

which took him from Oxford to Aylesbury, Buckinghamshire, in twenty minutes.

It is commonly asserted that Sadler had little formal education. He is frequently described as a pastry chef, which he undoubtedly was, but it is misleading to use this as an indication of any lack of learning on his part, the reality is that we do not know much about his early life. He was certainly a man with significant scientific ability and his early employment included being a laboratory assistant at Oxford University, which is said by some to be where he first experimented with gas filled balloons.

Perhaps the most striking thing about Sadler's career as a balloonist is that it went on for so long. It was a dangerous calling. Rozier, one of the first to fly, also became one of the first to die in an aviation accident. Along with his companion Pierre Romain he was killed when his balloon crashed at Wimereux in the Pas-de-Calais during an attempt to fly across the English Channel. A number of early aeronauts met a similar end to their adventurous lives.

By contrast, Sadler achieved more than fifty ascents, but these were not without incident. He once almost drowned in the Irish Sea, and suffered serious injuries on another occasion when his balloon was dragged along the ground by the wind over a distance of some two miles. Tragically, his younger son Windham Sadler was killed in a ballooning accident in 1824, but James Sadler survived him, dying on 28 March 1828.

It follows from the above that ballooning was topical in the early nineteenth century and it became inevitable that science fiction would take up the challenge that this offered. Gas rather than gansas might now transport a man to the Moon; indeed, a correspondent to a newspaper as early as August 1784, fearing that the new technology might prove a threat to vested interests, had suggested that there was talk of a petition 'praying that Balloon owners may be restricted from taking passengers, except to the Moon.'[4]

A Visit to the Lunar Sphere was submitted to the editors of *Blackwood's Edinburgh Magazine* anonymously in 1820, and its author remained unidentified when it was published. In essence, it takes the form of an amusing update of Godwin's *The Man in the Moone*, but instead of an involuntary ascent to the moon by bird-power there is an unplanned visit there in a balloon. The accidental astronaut on this occasion is a Doctor Heidelberg[5] who the narrator has met during a visit to the Hague, where he shows Heidelberg some 'observations' made during a recent voyage into the Arctic, from which we may deduce that the narrator is a seafarer. Heidelburg is not much impressed by the observations:

'Pretty discoveries, indeed," said the Doctor, for an inhabitant of this globe; but had they possessed the advantage of a lunar view of these continents, we should see a very different account of them.'

He then goes on to tell the story of his 'last aeronautic excursion', which he claims had taken him to the Moon when he 'inadvertently set off with too much inflammable air'. Knocked unconscious during the flight by 'a shower of meteoric stones' he comes round on the lunar surface where he finds that: 'Nothing could be more enchanting than the surrounding scenery.' There are poplars, elms, oaks, cedars and fields of waving corn; along with birds and a flock of sheep. Quickly setting about some scientific tasks he finds himself approached by a seemingly human creature – who

---

[4] Smith, p.61.
[5] Initially referred to as 'Professor Heidelbergus', perhaps a jibe at those who Latinised their names, as was once common among European academics.

helpfully produces a theodolite. His new companion, Zuloc, is a Lunarian. The Lunarians possess telescopes of astonishing power, through which 'towns and rivers, fleets and armies' on earth can be clearly seen. They have also perfected a process of capturing light in order to induce darkness, by bottling the rays of the sun after passing them through a prism, and have found a way of achieving perpetual motion, harnessing it in order to complete tasks in ultra-short time. The Lunarians, like Godwin's Lunars, live to a great age. The author has some fun with this: his account includes a description of the educational programmes provided for forty and fifty year old children.

There are other ideas taken from *The Man in the Moone*, including a pigment of Godwin's imagination, a colour existing on the Moon that is not seen on Earth. *A Visit to the Lunar Sphere* tells us that all colours exist only in the imagination.

As we have seen, the author of *A Visit to the Lunar Sphere* did not identify himself at the time of its publication. When he signed off his story he simply called himself 'A Midshipman': but he assured his readers that they could 'Depend on hearing from me again next month'. Perhaps he would then reveal his identity. If his readers hoped for this they were to be disappointed, the next communication from the author did not come until four months later, in the form of a letter to the magazine stating that it was from 'The Man in the Moon': convincing evidence one would think of his inspiration for *A Visit to the Lunar Sphere*, but still not revealing to readers who he was.

Andrew Barger has shown in his *Mesaerion: The Best Science Fiction Stories 1800 - 1849* that the author of *A Visit to the Lunar Sphere* was Captain Frederick Marryat, who went on to write *Peter Simple; or, the Adventures of a Midshipman* and other popular novels, including *The Children of the New Forest*.

A Visit to the Lunar Sphere is probably Marryat's earliest work of fiction. His link with *Blackwood's Edinburgh Magazine* seems to have followed his marriage to Catherine Shairp, the daughter of a Scot, in 1819, shortly after which he is known to have had dealings with the editors of the periodical. But he was not in Scotland, or England, when his story was published, he was at sea. Either he left the manuscript with the editors for consideration of publication while he was away or simply sent it back to them from wherever he was. He was the captain of a ship called the *Beacon*, which may explain why his promise to readers that they would hear further from him within a month was not fulfilled, the *Beacon* was by then destined for Saint Helena.

As is well known, Napoleon had been sent to the island in 1815 and security surrounding his presence there was intense. This included the need for ships to be on continuous duty offshore. The *Beacon* was to become a Saint Helena guardship, although this was not what Marryat had hoped for. He had a considerable interest in science, albeit that he treated it lightly in *A Voyage to the Lunar Sphere*, and his ambition was to be engaged by the Admiralty on a voyage of discovery, perhaps with a scientific purpose. It is interesting to note that he had been elected as a member of the Royal Society for Scientific Knowledge in 1819, the very body his character Doctor Heidelberg in *A Visit to The Lunar Sphere* is due to lay his findings before as the story finishes, which provides still more evidence of Marryat's authorship. Marryat certainly read widely and as his first work of fiction was based on a story partly set on Saint Helena, we may reasonably speculate that he read *The Man in the Moone* as he prepared for his voyage to the island.

In the event, the most significant incident arising during this part of Marryat's life had nothing to do with science, real or fictional. Marryat was at Saint Helena when Napoleon died on 5 May 1821 and his sketch of Napoleon's body, made at Longwood House a few hours after the great man's death, became famous. It was Marryat who was entrusted with the captaincy of the *Rosario* to which he transferred from the *Beacon* and it was the *Rosario* that brought the despatches back to England telling of Napoleon's death. For the moment, Marryat was not known by the public as an author, but we will now turn to him in that role, placing it in its Saint Helena context.

V

The Flying Dutchman

The tale of the *Flying Dutchman* is well known and continues to be retold to this day, including in the popular film series *Pirates of the Caribbean*. The original story is that of a ship that rounds the Cape of Good Hope on a return voyage from the Far East. Apparently lost, it becomes destined to sail for ever in a South Atlantic limbo, with its ghostly re-appearances becoming a portent of doom for other vessels.

The earliest version of the tale in English is found in *Travels in Various Parts of Europe, Asia, and Africa, During a Series of Thirty Years and Upwards*, published in 1790;[1] the memoirs of a John Macdonald, born in Scotland in 1741. His brief account of the *Flying Dutchman*, which his ship encounters during a voyage from Cape Town to Saint Helena, is as follows:

'The weather was so stormy that the sailors said they saw the Dutchman. The common story is that this Dutchman came to the Cape in distress of weather, and wanted to get into harbour, but could not get a pilot to conduct her, and was

---

[1] Reprinted in *Memoirs of an XVIII Century Footman*, ed. John Beresford, 1927.

lost; and that ever since, in very bad weather, her vision appears. The sailors fancy that, if you would hail her, she would answer like another vessel. At length we got into the trade-winds, and had fine weather, so that we hardly shifted a sail for two weeks, when the ship's company had ease after hard work. We came down with pleasure to St. Helena, and stopped ten days.'[2]

From then on, the story of the Flying Dutchman was firmly embedded in Saint Helena's history.

The *Flying Dutchman* story first appeared in fiction in May 1821, in the form of a short story published in *Blackwood's Edinburgh Magazine*, the publication which Marryat's *A Voyage to the Lunar Sphere* had appeared in the previous year. In *Vandecken's Message Home, or the Tenacity of Natural Affection*, a ship that has rounded the Cape of Good Hope experiences difficult weather, including lightning, and encounters the *Flying Dutchman*, the captain of which attempts to pass letters over for forwarding to long dead addressees in Amsterdam. The acceptance of these, according to the established beliefs of those on board, can only lead to disaster. The frightened sailors refuse them but then find that the letters have been left on the deck of their ship as the *Flying Dutchman* disappears. Throwing them overboard is, according to nautical superstition, as dangerous as accepting them, but good fortune intervenes: the letters are swept into the sea by the elements and the ship escapes the threatening experience unscathed. We are not told where the ship was next headed, but almost inevitably its next port of call would have been Saint Helena. The author of the story was John Howison, an employee of the East India Company. He would have known of the conventional route via Saint Helena taken by ships at

---

[2] P. 171.

that time. *Vandecken's Message Home* established all the essentials of the *Flying Dutchman* tale, which was destined to become regularly revisited in science fiction thereafter.

The story of the *Flying Dutchman* was frequently linked with travelling to or from Saint Helena and it quickly became a part of the island's folklore. It was also the expectation of people back in England that travellers returning from a Saint Helena voyage would give an account of a sighting of the *Flying Dutchman*, even if sometimes told with tongue firmly set in cheek. Charles S. Dixon provides an example of this in his *Nautical Reminiscences of an Interesting Voyage to Saint Helena*, published in 1833:

'As the wine had circulated rather freely, one of the company facetiously inquired of me, if I had ever encountered the "Flying Dutchman." I replied in the affirmative; and I stamped my assertion with a still more astonishing degree of interest, by informing them, that I actually was the officer who, during a heavy storm of thunder and lightning, was carried on the top of one high sea, while in the jolly boat, right onto the quarter-deck of the Flying Dutchman; that I then in reality took dispatches off the drum-head of the capstan, directed to merchants in Amsterdam, who had been dead some 200 years; next positively launched my boat, and by taking advantage of a counter sea, thus reached my vessel in safety. Because there appeared some slight degree of improbability in the tale, they very politely christened me "The Flying Dutchman," by which title I have been pretty generally known ever since.'[3]

This assumed that both Dixon's dinner party friends and his readers were familiar with the story which, as in Howison's

---

[3] P. 94.

Vandecken's Message Home, included that the ghostly crew of the *Flying Dutchman* would attempt to pass messages for forwarding to the long dead. It also shows that the *Flying Dutchman* story was by then considered to have as much to do with Saint Helena as with the Cape, to which, significantly, Howison's voyage had not taken him: it was undertaken solely for the purpose of transporting goods, sixty fresh soldiers for the garrison and a new governor, Brigadier-General Charles Dallas, to Saint Helena. The route taken by Howison's ship was via the Cape Verde Islands and the small, rocky archipelago of Trinidade and Martin Vaz, which is 1,580 miles west of Saint Helena.

Dixon's tale may have been largely told for amusement but some voyagers to or from Saint Helena succumbed to the temptation to give an account of an experience involving the *Flying Dutchman* that was intended to be taken seriously, and some of the stories may have genuinely reflected what the observers believed themselves to have seen. An instance of this is given in Martin Montgomery's *History of the British Colonies*, completed in 1831:

'I avail myself of this opportunity to state, in confirmation of what I remarked, under the Cape of Good Hope chapter, in reference to the clearness of the atmosphere [in Saint Helena],[4] and the phenomenon of the 'Flying Dutchman,' that Sir Charles Forbes had, a few weeks since, a letter from a lady passenger on board the Buckinghamshire Indiaman (which conveyed the Right Hon. R. Grant to Bombay), describing the appearance of the 'Flying Dutchman' to the Buckinghamshire on her voyage from St. Helena to the Cape.

---

[4] Which Montgomery had placed in his Cape chapter.

The Dutchman was visible to all on board, bearing down, with all sail set, *against the wind!*'

The final italics and exclamation mark appear in the original, reflecting that this was something strange. We have here the sighting of what appears to be a ghostly ship, seemingly brought about by a combination of the power of suggestion in the human mind and the atmospheric conditions prevailing at the time. Here it seems to have been 'the clearness of the atmosphere' that resulted in its appearance.

In 1839, Captain Marryat, who we have already come across as a writer of science fiction and as a visitor to Saint Helena, produced his novel *The Phantom Ship*. It was not his best received work and was panned by the critics at the time. The central character is Philip Vandercken, the son of the captain of the phantom ship of the title, which we soon learn is the *Flying Dutchman*. Philip goes to sea in an effort to free his father from the perpetual voyage that he is trapped in, armed with a holy relic left to him by his late mother. Saint Helena is 'the island' in what follows:

'Again they passed the Cape without meeting the Phantom Ship; and Philip was not only in excellent health, but in good spirits. As they lay becalmed, with the island in sight, they observed a boat pulling towards them, and in the course of three hours she arrived on board.'

The occupants of the boat, but not their ship, have survived an encounter off Saint Helena with the *Flying Dutchman* and 'There are twenty men on deck to tell the story.' The 'Ghost Ship' had appeared in a 'ball of mist' during an otherwise clear night. Voices were heard but little was seen other than 'the loom of her hull.' When a gun was discharged, 'the fog and all disappeared as if by magic, and the whole horizon was clear, and there was nothing to be seen. The ship from which all of this had been observed then took in water and was lost. According to its mate, the vessel they had come across 'is well known – it is called the *Flying Dutchman*.'

In the final appearance of Marryat's phantom ship it rises from the depths until it floats on the surface of the sea:

> 'On the beam of the ship, not more than two cables' length distant, they beheld, slowly rising out of the water, the tapering mast-head and spars of other vessel. She rose and rose gradually; her topmasts and top-sail yards, with the sails set, next made their appearance; higher and higher she rose up from the element. Her lower masts and rigging, and, lastly, her hull showed itself above the surface. Still she rose up till her ports, with her guns, and at last the whole of her floatage was above water, and hove-to. "Holy Virgin!" exclaimed the captain, breathless, "I have known ships to go down, but never to come up before."

The apparent rising of the ship into view is something that we will come back to later when looking at the various naturally occurring circumstances that have been credited with giving rise to the myth.

The *United Services Journal and Naval and Military Magazine* of 1841 records a non-fictional experience at Saint Helena, in a sea mist:

> 'We sailed in the direction due west all the night; and just as the day dawned, I was on deck, it having been announced that we were close in with the land. The scene was curious: the ship seemed to be nearly becalmed, under a huge black wall of rock, of uncertain heights and dimensions, as the summit was covered with a thick fog; at a small distance was seen one of our cruising frigates, appearing in the uncertain

light, like the phantom of a ship, that might have passed in the heated imagination as the *Flying Dutchman*.'

Here we have an observation in factually reported as opposed to fictional conditions that might produce the illusion of a phantom ship, if only to a receptive mind. Importantly, the writer sees it as relevant, if only as an aside, to include this as part of an account of the arrival of a vessel at Saint Helena.

As we have seen, the conditions for the *Flying Dutchman*'s appearance range from stormy seas to flat calms, from clear visibility to thick fog, making it difficult to point to a single naturally occurring phenomenon which can explain the origin of the legend. But it is the role of fiction to fictionalise and many eventual embellishments can flow from a single original source. Several types of optical illusion come into play – both as a starting point for the idea and as the inspiration for later adaptations of it.

The mists at Saint Helena are less frequent than those at the Cape. Anyone who has arrived at Cape Town by ship in the early morning is likely to have seen the thick sea mist that is commonly experienced there. It is caused by the cold Benguela current of the Atlantic meeting up with the relatively warm land mass of the Cape, the eastern side of which benefits from the Agulhas current of the Indian Ocean. It produces an eerie effect, particularly when another vessel, such as the pilot boat, comes briefly into view and disappears again. A fixed object, such as Table Mountain, may be seen for a few moments and then seems to have significantly changed position when it next appears, the ship from which it is being observed having moved, imperceptibly to the observer, who is then confused by the shifting mist. Such effects conjure up spectres.

At the other end of the scale, we have rough sea conditions. These had a profound effect on those who were forced to endure them in the days of sail, with sailors often fearing for their lives. But what causes a ghostly ship to appear in these circumstances? Probably, it is the simple fact that other vessels may be spotted and quickly lost sight of again. Glimpsed for no more than a moment, a seaman telling his story of it, perhaps more than a little embellished when recounted over a grog or two, could report a phantom vessel.

There is also a phenomenon known as 'looming', the dictionary definition of which is promising: 'appear as a vague form, especially one that is large or threatening'. Its synonyms are even more so, including 'emerge, appear, become visible, come into view, take shape, materialize, reveal itself, appear indistinctly, come to light, take on a threatening shape, be ominously close, threaten, be threatening, menace.' But what does this amount to in science? In the late eighteenth century, William Latham wrote his *Account of a Singular Instance of Atmospherical Refraction*, which he set out in a letter to the Rev. Henry Whitfield on 1 August 1797. On 26 July of that year Latham had been sitting in the dining room of his home in Hastings when at about 5.00 p.m. he became aware of a number of people running down to the seafront. The coast of France, not normally visible from Hastings, was in full view and 'gradually emerging more elevated, and approaching nearer, as it were'. Local sailors and fishermen were able to point out and name the places that could be seen, which they 'were accustomed to visit', including some in the vicinity of Boulogne, forty-six miles away. Latham wrote that even without the use of a telescope:

'I could very plainly see the cliffs on the opposite coast: which, at the nearest part, are between forty and fifty miles distant, and are not to be discerned, from that low situation, by the aid of the best glasses. They appeared to be only a few miles off, and seemed to extend for some leagues along the coast.'

Moving to higher ground nearby, Latham noted that features along the French Coast, such as fishing boats at anchor and individual buildings on shore, could be seen as far west as Dieppe, which is sixty-eight miles from Hastings. Latham was a serious scientist and he presented his letter to a meeting of the Royal Society on 10 May 1798. It was later published in the society's *Philosophical Transactions*. There was no heated imagination at work here, this seems to be an early account of looming – the abnormally large refraction of an object that increases its apparent elevation and appears to bring it closer to the observer.

The optical illusion known as the Fata Morgana must also be considered, as it is believed by many to offer the key to the origin of the *Flying Dutchman* legend. It is the Italian name for Morgan le Fay of the Arthurian stories, given to the phenomenon because it was believed to result from her use of her magical powers in the Strait of Messina, between Sicily and the Italian mainland, creating the effect of land or other objects being suspended in the air. It has a high profile in literature. Henry Wadsworth Longfellow led the way in 1873 by publishing his poem simply entitled *Fata Morgana*. Whatever its literary merits, it seems that this was less than sound scientifically. An authority on the subject has shown that Longfellow's description was actually of the Fata Morgana's poor relation, the 'inferior' mirage commonly reported as a phenomenon in deserts. The real thing is a superior one in which the image rises into the sky – where it has the unfortunate habit of inverting itself. Upside down ships do not much feature in reported appearances of the *Flying Dutchman* so it seems reasonable to discard this as an explanation. My personal favourite from among the above is looming, which offers us objects rising into view and seeming to be closer than they are. It provides a suitable level of astonishment, as in the case of Marryat's captain in *The Phantom Ship*, who has never before seen a vessel rise from the depths.

It seems likely that Marryat's *Phantom Ship* was inspired by his visit to Saint Helena in 1821. He would have been aware of the *Flying Dutchman* story when he undertook his voyage there, perhaps before his departure from England he would also have heard of a strange occurrence there in 1818. In September of that year an unidentified vessel was seen close to Saint Helena. Attempts by British ships to investigate it simply resulted in its disappearance. Further pursuits, continuing into October, produced the same outcome. Eventually, the ship was seen no more, slipping away with its identity still undiscovered. When Marryat arrived at the island in 1821 it was a mystery that remained unsolved, although there had been speculation about it in the English press.[5] The truth did not emerge until some thirty years later (well after the publication of the *Phantom Ship*), when an account of a Lieutenant Thomas Sheffield, the second in command of the spectral vessel, revealed that it was an American privateer operating out of Buenos Aires, and that freeing Napoleon had been under active consideration by those on board. It is to Napoleon that we will now turn.

---

[5] *Courier*, London, November 16, 1818. Cited by Emilio Ocampo in The Emperor's Last Campaign, p.467.

VI

Napoleon's Alternative History

Napoleon died on Saint Helena on 5 May 1821. There has been much speculation as to what might have become a somewhat different history of his life had he not ended his days there. Alternative history ('alternate' in America) is a recognised branch of science fiction: the past, like the future, can offer differing outcomes in the imagination. Much of what will happen in the future is far from certain and events that are fixed for all time because they have already occurred were not necessarily bound to have turned out as they did. The major events of history seem to us to have been inevitable for no greater reason than we know how they ended, or, at least, we so believe. As Napoleon is famously supposed to have said, 'History is a set of lies agreed upon'.[1] Outcomes often hang on a thread and had things turned out differently Napoleon might well have won the Battle of Waterloo and not been sent to Saint Helena. Many books have been written on this particular subject; and some have gone even further. In *Histoire de la Monarchie universelle: Napoleon et la conquete du monde*

---

[1] In fact, there is no record of him having said this, at least not in these words. In dictating his memoirs to Las Cases he did describe history as a fable.

(1812-1832) [*History of the Universal Monarchy: Napoleon and the Conquest of the World (1812-1832)*] by Louis-Napoleon Geoffroy-Chateau (1836), the Battle of Waterloo did not even take place, with Napoleon having prevailed in Russia in 1812 and gone on to take Britain in 1814. Domination of the world was his final flourish, with the inevitability that French became the universal language. In this outcome, Waterloo would have simply remained a little-known village in what is now Belgium, today a town with a population of around thirty-thousand people.

The Napoleon Options, edited by Jonathan North, provides an anthology of alternative outcomes of Napoleon's military adventures, including success in Egypt. The choice is seemingly endless. Alternative histories of Napoleon are, unsurprisingly, the runaway winners of this sub-genre of science fiction in France and account for more than ten per cent of alternative history sales worldwide.

It would be inconvenient for the present book had Napoleon not fought (and lost) at Waterloo and been exiled to Saint Helena. In the immediate aftermath of the battle, Napoleon climbed into his carriage and fled the field. His first instinct was to cling to power, he had survived military setbacks before. Arriving in Paris he announced that he had achieved a great victory; which, if it had been true, hardly explained his presence back there. He was referring to Ligny, where he had defeated the Prussians, but not decisively. They were able to regroup and arrive at Waterloo two days later, thus securing the outcome in the battle that mattered. With a resumption of power proving impossible he considered his other options, including the idea of going to America. To this end he sought a passport, a promise of an unimpeded voyage across the Atlantic. The Duke of Wellington responded on 28 June 1815 that he had 'no authority from his government, or from the Allies, to give any answer to the demand of a passport or assurances of safety for Napoleon Buonaparte and his family to pass to the United States of America.' There was an element of slight in this: 'Buonaparte' was the Corsican spelling of Napoleon's family name.

Passport or no passport, the idea of going to America was realistic, as Napoleon's brother Joseph was to demonstrate. Napoleon himself travelled south in France to fine tune his plans, expecting the arrival of 'horses and other objects calculated to promote his comfort in his new existence.' On 3 July he arrived at Rochefort, where the French frigates *Saale* and *Méduse* awaited him, but the winds and a British blockade were aligned against him. An alternative option was to place his fate in the hands of the captain of a corsair vessel, the *Bayadère*, then anchored in the Gironde estuary, south of Rochefort. Captain Charles Baudin was there, ready and willing to take on the challenge, with other vessels that might provide a distraction when the attempt was made. Uncharacteristically, Napoleon did not seize the moment. He was reluctant to meet Baudin's requirement to sail with only two or three companions and a restricted amount of baggage. A Danish brig, the *Magdaleine*, competed with the *Bayadère* for the honour, but was also rejected.

On 8 July, under pressure from the provisional government in Paris, which had given him twenty-four hours to leave the country, Napoleon proceeded to Ile-d'Aix. This sealed his fate: the *Bellerophon*, a frigate of the Royal Navy, was there. The task of dealing with Napoleon then fell to Frederick Maitland, the captain of the *Bellerophon*. Maitland gave his opinion that Napoleon would be treated in accordance with the laws of England, a view (probably honestly held) that Maitland later much regretted. He believed with hindsight that he had behaved in a dishonourable way towards a man for whom he had the utmost respect and more than a little sympathy. In the event, Napoleon was not to be allowed access to the English courts. With the now captive Napoleon on board, Maitland made the crossing to England, first anchoring his ship at Torbay and then off Plymouth; but Napoleon was not permitted to go ashore. Had he been permitted to do so, or if the relevant legal papers had been served while he was within territorial waters, he would have been within the jurisdiction of the High Court in London and might well have been freed. Contrary to what he had been told by Maitland, he was not to be treated in accordance with the laws of England. Napoleon was being held as a prisoner of war and as such was entitled to be released when the war was over, which it clearly was, even if a war had been declared in the first place – England was fighting Napoleon on behalf of the Bourbons, it was not at war with France.

At Plymouth, on 31 July, Napoleon was informed that he was to be taken to Saint Helena, then a colony of the East India Company, where the writ of the English High Court did not run. He was transferred to HMS *Northumberland* for the voyage to Saint Helena. The warrant that Admiral Cockburn held for this was unequivocal – Napoleon was a prisoner of war. Hudson Lowe's warrant when he took over from Cockburn on the island in 1816 was similarly expressed and duly copied into the local deeds register, complete with a pen and ink rendering of its seal. The register survives to this day. For the moment the legal niceties consequent upon its wording were evaded. The problems posed as to the legality of Napoleon's detention on the island had to be settled by two Acts of Parliament in 1816, the second of which indemnified from legal process all persons who in detaining Napoleon had acted in ways 'which may not be strictly justified by Law'. Severe penalties were provided, including death for those who might be tempted to assist in his escape from the island. But was escape possible? There were many who thought so, including Lord Bathurst, the Minister for War and Colonies. Nothing could be ruled out. Plans for an escape, real and imagined, were rife; and perhaps more likely to succeed than we now realise.

Once it is accepted that Napoleon was held prisoner on the island his detention there gives rise to a further idea that has also been explored in alternative histories: what if he had then escaped, as he had from Elba? The accepted view, again largely reliant on the apparent inevitability of history, remains that slipping away from Saint Helena was not a serious option for Napoleon. In any event, mainstream history tells us that he would not have gone along with any proposal for it anyway – he is said to have pinned his hopes on a dignified release. But perhaps his apparent disinclination to escape was part of the plan, a subterfuge. He did, after all, have something of a past on this, although the escape from Elba had been relatively easy, Napoleon simply sailed away while the British officer responsible for keeping him there had gone off to spend time with his mistress on the Italian mainland. Saint Helena though was different, not least because of its remoteness and the number of soldiers stationed there. The Royal Navy dominated the seas and had vessels on continuous alert around the island. In addition to this, Hudson Lowe, the Governor of the island at the time, was resolute to the point of obsession in his determination to fulfil his duty.

Nevertheless, a variety of proposals were put forward as ways of securing Napoleon's release and, along with imagined ones, were taken seriously by those charged with his detention. These ranged from a full-scale invasion of the island from South America to using one or more of a number of then cutting-edge scientific advances to simply spirit him away.

The ideas for Napoleon's release did include an invasion of Saint Helena by sympathetic forces, but 'smuggling a silken ladder to him, hidden in a teapot'[2], which is also said to have been proposed, seems a little fanciful. Aside from a change of heart in London, which might have allowed him to leave the island with dignity, we may reasonably speculate that invasion would have been Napoleon's first preference: it is unlikely that he would have had much enthusiasm for dangling over Saint Helena's awesome cliffs on a silken ladder. Under very different circumstances he had advanced plans for taking the island by force in 1804, and it follows that much was already known about how this might be achieved. Many of his officers and men had gone to South America to take part in the wars of independence against Spain, and they were much in need of a figurehead to carry this aim forward.

Was the idea of rescuing Napoleon by seizing the island realistic? Contrary to popular belief, Saint Helena was vulnerable to invasion. The Dutch had taken it from the English on New Year's Eve, 1672, and the English had recovered it from them a few months later. Both sides in that conflict were able to effect a landing there while it was held by opposing forces. Neither the Dutch nor the English came ashore at a recognised landing spot: the Dutch used Swanley Valley, difficult to access even today, and the English scaled a cliff.[3] It was these incidents in its past that more than justified the number of British soldiers deployed there during Napoleon's detention on the island. When better fortified and garrisoned, as it was by 1815, Saint Helena offered a

---

[2] Simon Winchester, Outposts, p. 144. This is said to have been the idea of Saul Solomon, a merchant on the island at the time. Solomon and Co. remains in business on Saint Helena to this day.

[3] The spot is still known today as 'Holdfast Tom' after the man who climbed it and let a rope down for his fellows. It is only a short walk from Longwood House, where Napoleon lived for most of his time on the island.

formidable challenge to any would be invader: but recent scientific and technical advances offered a number of other options, several of which were seriously put forward – including utilising a steamship, a balloon, one or more submarines, or any combination of these.

Escape from the windward side of the island would have been difficult in a sailing vessel. For this reason, it was the least guarded part of the shores. But what about steam? A vessel propelled by steam power would be able to make its way into the wind far more easily than a pursuing ship of the Royal Navy relying on sails. Was it feasible? We do know that it was proposed. An American, Robert Fulton, had pioneered the technology and developed viable steam vessels. He offered the technology to both Britain and France, but without success, and enjoyed his greatest commercial success back in his native United States, where Joseph Bonaparte was offering a million dollar reward for his brother's rescue from Saint Helena, although Fulton does not appear to have been tempted by this. The technology though could be used by others. A steam vessel, the *Rising Star*, was commissioned by a disenchanted British admiral, Lord Cochrane, who was prepared to assist in Napoleon's escape. It was built in England; but there it remained, with engine problems and under surveillance by the authorities. It simply languished in the Thames for more than three years.

As we have already seen, balloons had arrived on the scene as a means of manned flight, and France led the world in the development of these. Might escape by balloon have been an option? The Royal Navy had a considerable presence around Saint Helena. Vessels approaching the island could also be seen at a considerable distance from several of the island's many high points: the peaks rise to a height of two thousand six hundred and ninety-seven feet.[4] An unnoticed approach and departure would be difficult to achieve by conventional means. In order to escape, Napoleon would have get to a viable and unguarded landing spot without detection. But a balloon would be able to make landfall anywhere on the island and, in favourable conditions, quickly carry him to a ship waiting out of sight. This was first suggested as early as 1816 but it is a proposal put to Napoleon's brother Joseph in 1818 which is notable. The main problem with balloons was steering them, but Jean Hippolyte Colins believed that he had come up with a solution to this. He put it to Joseph, who rejected it on the basis that Napoleon did not wish to be associated with an attempt 'of this nature'. It seems from this that it may have been the means rather than the principle that Napoleon was opposed to. His own experience with balloons had not been encouraging and the French balloon corps, the second company of which had accompanied him during his occupation of Egypt, was disbanded in 1799. Nevertheless, for a writer of alternative history, Napoleon escaping from Saint Helena by balloon would be a tempting idea, and there were other proposals worthy of similar consideration by a writer.

Submarines, frequently called 'submersibles' at the time, had been around for a while, and the word 'submarine' had been in use since 1648.[5] Edmond Halley built one, and

---

[4] *Diana's Peak.*

[5] German U-Boats later derived their name from the word 'unterseeboot' – undersea boat. In 1941, the U-68 demonstrated how easy it is for a submarine to approach Saint Helena without detection. On 22 October of that year the U-68 torpedoed the *RFA Darkdale*, which was at anchor in James Bay, with tragic consequences – forty-one of her crew were killed. The ship, a tanker, broke in two and now rests on the bottom, a short distance off shore. It is an official war grave. The names of those lost may be seen on the Cenotaph situated on the seafront below Jamestown. The wreck of the *Darkdale* is within swimming distance of the shore.

descended in it, albeit in the relative safety of the Thames. Halley's could even make some progress below the surface, but not over great distances. It also required a highly visible surface vessel from which to operate. The further development of submersibles was a task that fell to others.

It should not surprise us that an escape plan using a submarine was among those put forward for Napoleon's rescue from Saint Helena. As with a balloon, it would have overcome the problem of approaching and leaving the island without detection; or, at least, it could dive and avoid interception by a surface ship if interrupted in its task.

Reasonably efficient submersibles had been devised and Napoleon was familiar with them from his days back in France. As with balloons, he had not been much impressed. A demonstration of their possibilities had been put on for him in Paris, but the prototype, which submerged in the Seine in his presence, leaked badly. In spite of this less than encouraging episode, technology had moved on: so much so that Napoleon might well have been prepared to give due consideration to escape from Saint Helena in a submarine. As with the balloon option, there were serious proposals for this. In 1817, William Balcombe, whose hospitality Napoleon had enjoyed during his first few weeks on Saint Helena, informed Napoleon that French officers planning to rescue him using a submarine had been arrested in Brazil. A more advanced plan, in 1820, was later revealed by Sir Walter Scott, in his *The Life of Napoleon Buonaparte, Emperor of the French. With a Preliminary View of the French Revolution*. This involved Napoleon's doctor, Barry O'Meara, who had been expelled from Saint Helena in August 1818. Back in England, O'Meara met up with Thomas Johnstone, who had worked some years before with the Robert Fulton of steamboat fame, a man who also designed submersibles. Johnstone's was twenty-seven feet long and five feet wide, a considerable craft, and was also able to operate on the surface under sail. It was said to be able to submerge for up to twelve hours and progress under water at a speed of four knots (about four and a half miles an hour). Its main problem was the unlikelihood of it being able to get to Saint Helena without the assistance of a significantly larger surface vessel. But O'Meara got as far as commissioning an apparently suitable submersible, at a cost of around £15,000 (an enormous sum at the time). Depending on which version of events one reads it was built at Blackwall Reach on the Thames, downstream of London, or it was built upriver but destroyed at Blackwall Reach when an attempt was made to take it through to the sea. It is at this point that we must accept the difficulty of separating fact from fiction. *Scenes and Stories by a Clergyman in Debt*, was published in 1835. Its account of the plan to use a submersible to free Napoleon differs from Sir Walter Scott's. The author writes what purports to be the true story, having been told it by Johnstone while they were both in a debtor's prison: but it has been suggested that *Scenes and Stories* was actually written by Johnstone in an effort to put the record straight following Scott's version. This, though, is not to say that *Scenes and Stories* contains the truth either. Johnstone had a long history of dishonesty as well as debt. A bit of science fiction, an apparently fully formulated plan to free Napoleon with the new technology of a submarine, was not beyond him. That said, if it was indeed part of a genuine plot, he did have some impressive credentials, having twice escaped from prison himself. Whatever the truth of all this, we do know that Napoleon was not freed by this or any other means: but science fiction is fully entitled to tell us otherwise.

Recent works of alternative fiction have tended to concentrate less on the means by which Napoleon might have escaped from Saint Helena than on what he might have gone on to do had this been achieved. In *Napoleon in America*, Shannon Selin tells of Napoleon's military success in Texas following his escape from the island. Selin is a tireless compiler of facts about Napoleon's life, as is amply and informatively demonstrated by her website,[6] which contains a wealth of information about him: but she is sparing in her novel as to the means of Napoleon's fictional departure from Saint Helena. The only hint given in her book is when the then governor of the island, Hudson Lowe, considers what might have gone wrong in his plans to prevent Napoleon getting away, at which point he includes a 'submersible' among the several plans of which he had been forewarned.

In Simon Ley's *The Death Of Napoleon* the treatment is entirely different. In this, Napoleon simply escapes by sea as a double takes his place at Longwood. The detail of this is avoided by a presumably fictional reference on the first page of the book in which we are told: 'How the Emperor's escape from St Helena eventually succeeded during the last stage of an extraordinarily ingenious plot, is a story that has already been narrated elsewhere (see 'the Prisoner of St Helena' in *Fireside Stories*, June/July 1904).' The book is both comic and tragic – and at times surreal. Napoleon revisits Waterloo, which has become a tourist attraction, and is later lured into an asylum in Paris where all the inmates are dressed as (and believe themselves to be) Napoleon. *The Death of Napoleon* was later adapted for the screen in the form of *The Emperor's New Clothes* (2001). Ley praised Ian Holm's playing of both Napoleon and his double but was left to 'dream of what could have been achieved had the producer and director bothered to read the book.' This seems a little unfair: while books largely

---

[6] Shannon Selin: *Imagining the Bounds of History*.

rely on the imagination of the reader, films visualise things for us. The film explored new ground, some of it dealing with what a reader of the book might reasonably have wished to know but does not find there. A reader is left unaware, for example, of how the duplicate Napoleon fared on Saint Helena, but the film has him (and Holm) revelling in the role – the opportunity presented for the same actor to play the two parts was too good to miss. The double enjoys his new life on the island and even takes over the narration of Napoleon's memoirs, with racy accounts of his love life included. There is nothing wrong with a film differing from the book on which it is based, these are different mediums. The history of science fiction shows us that there are things that can be portrayed in a film which are difficult to achieve in a novel: but, on the other hand, and sympathising with Ley, an element of subtlety may be lost in a film version of a book.

Carolyn McCrae's novel, *A Set of Lies*, also makes use of a double, but the purpose of the substitution in her book is to prevent Napoleon being sent to Saint Helena, not to free him from the island. This idea has some basis in fact. Joseph, Napoleon's older brother, offered himself as a double in order to enable Napoleon to escape from France to America in 1815. They were strikingly similar in appearance, with Joseph being only slightly taller and slimmer than his brother. In the event, it was Napoleon's surrender of himself at the Ile d'Aix that diverted attention from Joseph, enabling him to slip away from Bordeaux, arriving in America a free man at the end of August after a passage of thirty-four days.

VII
Alpha Centauri

Alpha Centauri is the description given to a constellation of stars that, apart from the Sun, are those closest to Earth. The group consists of three stars, Alpha Centauri A and B, which are relatively close together, and a detached one, Proxima Centauri. As viewed from Earth by the naked eye, Alpha Centauri A and B appear as a single star. Taken together, they would provide the third brightest star visible to us. Taken alone, Alpha Centauri A is the fourth brightest that can be seen from Earth.

In Ptolemy's time, the second century AD, Alpha Centauri was visible from his observatory at Alexandria, in Egypt, and he recorded his sighting of it. Importantly for what follows we should note that it can no longer be seen from that far North. This is due to what is termed 'proper motion', the movement of objects through space over an extended period of time. Today, it cannot be seen from within most of the Northern Hemisphere.

It was Robert Hues, mentioned earlier, perhaps a visitor to Saint Helena in 1588, who brought Alpha Centauri back to the attention of European astronomers, describing it in his *Tractus de Globis* of 1592. If Hues was indeed one of the first group of Englishmen to call at the island, having travelled on Thomas Cavendish's famous voyage around the globe, which had commenced in 1586, then he would have spent twelve days on Saint Helena, ample time during which to take advantage of its unique position and significantly better for purposes of observation than when on board a ship at sea. Certainly, it was Saint Helena that was later to provide a significant breakthrough in our knowledge of Alpha Centauri.

Brigadier-General Alexander Walker became governor of the island on 11 March 1823. With Napoleon less than two years dead and the naval and military forces consequently much diminished, the island had gone quickly from relative prosperity to hard times. Walker set about reviving things, concentrating on agriculture and education. One of his innovations was the founding of the Military Institution, offering young officers the opportunity of scientific instruction, notably in astronomy. This had a practical as well as academic purpose, it would enable accurate time to be established, enabling correction of the chronometers of ships calling at the island, an important factor in ensuring that they could better calculate their positions while at sea. To this end, an observatory was built at Ladder Hill, overlooking Jamestown, the foundation stone for which was laid on 13 September 1826. The building was completed in 1828 and Manuel Johnson, an officer in the Saint Helena Artillery, was given charge of it. Born at Macao, China, in 1805, Johnson was the son of an employee of the East India Company and had attended the company's training establishment in England. It is unlikely that the curriculum there offered much in the way of astronomical instruction but the study of mathematics was an essential part of artillery training, as it is in astronomy. His subsequent work at the Ladder Hill Observatory was of such an advanced level that in 1835 he won the Gold Medal of the

Royal Astronomical Society, for his *A Catalogue of 606 Principal Fixed Stars in the Southern Hemisphere: Deduced from Observations Made at the Observatory, St. Helena, from November 1829 to April 1833.* Importantly, for present purposes, he noted the 'high proper motion' of the Alpha Centauri system. Most stars are so remote from Earth that they appear motionless over long periods of time: high proper motion is important as an indicator of the observable movement of a star and, accordingly, its relative closeness to Earth. Almost inevitably, such proximity is of interest to writers of science fiction who wish to come up with fantastical stories of inter-galactic excursions. As Arthur C Clarke was to write in a letter to a friend:

'Beautiful night last night. Southern Cross (a very feeble constellation) just above the front gate, with Alpha Centauri beside it. It always gives me an odd feeling to look at Alpha and to realize that's the next stop.'[7]

Johnson shared his findings at the Ladder Hill Observatory with Thomas Henderson of the Royal Observatory at the Cape of Good Hope, in what has been described as:

'... an unexpected letter, received just a few weeks before he [Henderson] embarked on his voyage home from South Africa in 1833. The surprise missive that set Henderson on his path towards fame was written by Manuel Johnson, a member of the Saint Helena Artillery... an avid astronomer. Johnson had lived on the remote island in the South Atlantic for many years and had become a friend of Fearon Fallows,[8]

---

[7] In a 1955 letter to the British rocket scientist Val Cleaver.
[8] Fallows was the astronomer tasked with founding the observatory at the Cape of Good Hope. He was an ordained priest in the Church of England.

and had in fact visited the Cape Observatory on a number of occasions.'[9]

This resulted in the earliest successful measurement of what is termed 'stellar parallax', enabling the distance of Alpha Centauri from Earth to be ascertained. Johnson had made very accurate observations of the southern stars and his positional measurements, when compared with those of Abbé Nicolas-Louis de Lacaille some eighty years before during Lacaille's voyage on the *Le Glorieux*, showed that Alpha Centauri A must have a large proper motion.[10] As Johnson suggested in his letter to Henderson, Centauri A seemed to be a star close to Earth, for which a parallax displacement might be measurable. Achieving this was at the time a principal objective of astronomers. Henderson went on to do the necessary calculations but failed to publish his findings in time to gain full recognition of his efforts. Dithering through self-doubt for six years, because the figures that he had arrived at seemed to him to be too large, he was pipped at the post by others when it came to publication.

Alpha Centauri has been much visited in science fiction. It has just about everything required, including a likelihood of habitable planets, albeit currently too far away for any spacecraft from Earth to reach. *The Songs of Distant Earth* (1986), a novel by Arthur C. Clarke, tells of a colony established on a planet, Pasadena, in the Alpha Centauri system. Clarke regarded it as his personal favourite among his own novels. Alpha Centauri also featured in two episodes of *Star Trek* in 1967, *Tomorrow is Yesterday* and *Metamorphosis*. It has even inspired songs. *We Must Believe*

---

[9] Martin Beech, Alpha Centauri: Unveiling the Secrets of Our Nearest Stellar Neighbour. P. 32.
[10] Amounting to around 3.6 arc sec per year, which is of considerable significance to astronomers.

in Magic, which is about those on board a spaceship heading for Alpha Centauri, was the title track of a Crystal Gayle album in 1977 and was sung by her on the *Muppet Show*. Wikipedia lists around eighty poems, songs, films, television programmes, novels and computer games which tell of Alpha Centauri. Perhaps it is a sign of the times that it is currently most represented on Earth in computer games.

On Saint Helena there are now few traces of the important part the island played in unravelling the secrets of Alpha Centauri. The observatory on Ladder Hill was short lived and little of it remains today. When the Crown took over Saint Helena from the East India Company in 1834 the observatory was a significant casualty in a desire by the Crown to cut costs, the expenditure on it by then being around £300 a year. To justify closure of the observatory it was said at the time, despite clear evidence to the contrary, that the Crown's Commissioners 'had been unable to learn its establishment had been attended with any important result to science'.[11]

Fortunately, although the Crown removed much of what was of value from the observatory,[12] some of the instruments used there may still be seen on the island, notably a Barraud transit clock now in the front hallway of Plantation House, the residence of Saint Helena's governor. This has the characteristic three dials of such an instrument and is the twin of one returned to Greenwich in 1836 as part of the Crown's policy of asset stripping. The serial number of the clock at Plantation when compared to the one at Greenwich shows that the Plantation one dates back to at least 1827. Most of the other instruments from the observatory which remain on the island may be seen in the Jamestown Museum.

---

[11] Gosse, p.333.
[12] Some were sent to Canada.

The Time Office element of the facility at Ladder Hill is reflected in two other Barraud clocks, one of which is in the office at the museum and the other on the first floor landing at Plantation House (suitably co-located with a framed print of Big Ben). These date from around 1833.

Stripped of its instruments, the building that had housed the observatory simply became the mess-room of the Saint Helena Artillery. In 1878 it was reported that 'in the recesses formed for the shutters of the openings through which Johnson's transit used to peep, they stow wineglasses and decanters, and under the dome they play billiards!' These were the words of Mrs Gill, wife of Professor David Gill, in her memoir *Six Months in Ascension*. The Gills were visiting Saint Helena on their way to Ascension Island, in order to observe from there a near approach of Mars, their visit being intended to assist in the calculation of its distance from Earth. During the course of this enterprise, Professor Gill was informed of his appointment to the position of Her Majesty's Astronomer at the Cape of Good Hope, where he and Mrs Gill were to remain from 1879 to 1906. It was there that he played a part, perhaps unwittingly, in furthering the knowledge of Alpha Centauri, through the support and encouragement that he offered to Robert Innes, a fellow Scot. Innes's early life was spent as a wine merchant in Australia, but he had a considerable interest in astronomy, albeit that he had no formal education in it. Australia was a good place from which to gain knowledge of the southern stars. It was Sir David Gill, as he now was, and by this time HM Astronomer at the Royal Observatory, Cape of Good Hope, who invited Innes to join him there in 1894, and it was Innes who later discovered Proxima Centauri.[13] This is the third, somewhat faint star of

---

[13] In 1915. Gill did not live to share in the achievement, he died the previous year.

the Alpha Centauri group. To date, it is the closest star to Earth that has been identified.

In recent years, Proxima Centauri has attracted considerable interest as host to a planet, Proxima b. Speculation as to its habitability is based on a possibility that the twin requirements of a breathable atmosphere and the presence of water might be met there. It is, after all, closer to the Sun than anywhere else outside our own solar system. The popular press abounds with reports of the potential for life in the Alpha Centauri system. Typical of these is an item in *The Guardian*, in its edition of 24 August 2016: 'Discovery of potentially Earth-like planet Proxima b raises hopes for life.' The possibility, however, remains speculative, leaving science fiction as our only option at present. That said, there are plans to change this. NASA has announced a programme which will result in a probe being sent to Alpha Centauri in 2069, the hundredth anniversary of the first arrival of a man on the Moon. The voyage to Alpha Centauri will not be manned, the length of the flight and the lack of an opportunity to return to Earth being somewhat daunting. In the meantime, it must be left to science fiction to fill the gap in narratives of travel to the planets within its system.

VIII
Terraforming

John Young died on 5 January 2018, one of only twelve men to have walked on the Moon. His obituary in *The Daily Telegraph* told of his warnings about the future of Earth, based on the findings from twenty-five years of NASA research concerning the 'inevitability of future disasters involving giant volcanic activity, asteroid impacts and unpredictable solar activity'. We humans are, he said, 'in the deadly serious business of saving the species'. He suggested that the need was for studies of how best to modify the 'biospheres' of the Moon and Mars to make them habitable by humans.[1] The process he envisaged is known as terraforming, the dictionary definition of which is: 'Transform (a planet, environment, etc.) into something resembling the earth, esp. as regards suitability for human life.'[2] It is a term coined in 1942, in a work of science fiction, Jack Williamson's *Collision Orbit*.[3] Like science fiction itself, the concept pre-dated it acquiring a name, which is now commonly used by mainstream scientists.

H. G. Wells gave us the idea of terraforming, albeit in reverse, in his *The War of the Worlds*, in 1898. In this,

---

[1] *The Daily Telegraph*, 11 January 2018, p. 27.
[2] *The Shorter Oxford English Dictionary*, to which it was added in 1993.
[3] In the magazine *Astounding Science Fiction*.

Martians arrive on Earth, landing on Horsell Common, near Woking, Surrey, where Wells lived at the time. The Martians bring with them a red weed; which, at least in the short term, overcomes existing vegetation and grows rapidly wherever there is water. The Martians gain early victories over the British Army and Navy, but nature wins the day: the Martians are wiped out by pathogens, to which they have no immunity, and the red weed loses its own battle against earthly bacteria. This may give us a clue to the potential fate of ourselves and our terrestrial plant species if we are ever introduced elsewhere in the galaxy. But nothing limits the boundaries of science fiction, which has so often proved itself to eventually become science fact.

We know that other planets do not provide an environment within which humans could easily live, but is it possible to adapt them to meet our needs, as John Young suggested? We have been changing our earthly environment for as long as we have been around, notably when making the transition from hunter gatherers to farmers and later when exploiting the world's mineral resources. Today, our effect on the planet is fast becoming disastrous, both for ourselves and many other forms of life: it is not a matter of giant volcanic activity, asteroid impacts and unpredictable solar activity, but the use made of the planet by ourselves that threatens our future.

Historically, humans have usually chosen to live in the places on Earth that already meet or can easily be adapted to their needs and have not rushed to settle those inhospitable parts that seem to require, for human purposes, the creation of a completely new and viable ecosystem: but a notable proposal for this was made a little less than two hundred years ago, on Saint Helena's sister island of Ascension, which Charles Darwin visited after a short stay on Saint Helena.

Having by then largely completed his famous voyage on HMS *Beagle* Darwin had arrived at Saint Helena on 8 July 1836. He found it a place much changed from its natural condition when discovered by the Portuguese in 1502. The Portuguese had not settled the island but they released various non-native mammals there as a potential food source, to be exploited when they called, chief among these being goats.[4] The account of Thomas Cavendish's visit to the island in 1588 includes that:

'There are in this island of thousands of goats,... which are very wild: you shall see one or two hundred of them together, and sometimes you may behold them going in a flock almost a mile long.'[5]

The original, largely wooded landscape, quickly became degraded, leaving little more than some place names that survive to this day, such as Deadwood Plain. The efforts of settlers, who first arrived in 1659, simply served to aggravate the position, as they cleared their holdings for agriculture.

Darwin found little of interest on the island: he was there for only six days, too brief a time to observe what was still surviving there and much was missed by him. Nature is often stronger than we think and much of Saint Helena's endemic flora and fauna remained undetected by him. It is still surprisingly intact today. The island is home to more than five hundred species that are unique to it, including such things as

---

[4] There were no mammals naturally present on or at the island other than marine ones. Manatees, capable of clambering onto the shore, were reported by early visitors to be present, but they now survive only in the name of Manatee Bay.

[5] *The Prosperous Voyage of M. Candish esquire into the South sea, and so around about the circumference of the whole earth, begun in the year 1586.* 'Candish' was a variant of 'Cavendish' at the time.

the blushing snail (*Succinea sanctahelenae*) and the spiky yellow woodlouse (*Pseudolaureola atlantica*), although the survival of the giant earwig (*Labidura herculeana*), last seen alive in 1967, remains in question. As things stand, the last appearance of *Lapidura herculeana* was on a Saint Helena postage stamp issued in 1995. It was, and perhaps still is, the world's largest earwig, attaining a length of over three inches. Perhaps there is a future for the giant earwig if it keeps its head down for a while: although it may even help if it reveals itself, some Saint Helena species have been brought back from the brink through human intervention. In 1982, George Benjamin M.B.E., a self-taught Saint Helenian naturalist, discovered what, as far as we know, were then the last two endemic dwarf ebonies (*Trochetiopsis ebenus*), high up on the island. The progeny of these are now flourishing and examples can be seen in Britain, including at Kew Gardens and the Eden Project in Cornwall, as well as in pots on many a doorstep in Saint Helena and at various sites around the island where it has been successfully re-introduced. Identification of Saint Helena's endemics is ongoing and more will undoubtedly be found. Work is now being undertaken to restore the woodland, with the Millennium Forest, planted with endemic gumwoods, thriving in an area of the island that had previously been reduced to desert.

It was a naturally occurring desert, not yet interfered with by man, that Darwin was to find on Ascension Island. At the end of his all too brief visit to Saint Helena, Darwin set off for Ascension on 14 July 1836. Today, Ascension is closely associated, politically and culturally, with Saint Helena. I have described it above as its sister island, although it is situated over seven hundred miles away to its north-west. The histories of the two islands are inextricably linked. Although Ascension was discovered a year before Saint Helena, in 1501, it was not occupied until over three hundred years later when it was annexed by Britain as part of its strategy for preventing Napoleon's escape from Saint Helena. Its residents today are mostly Saint Helenians.

Ascension, like Saint Helena, is best described as a one-off sort of place: notable for being almost entirely destitute of water. Following its discovery, it was at first mostly left to itself, primarily because of this shortcoming. Unlike Saint Helena, it is a relatively modern island in geological terms, dating from around a million years ago, and has had insufficient time to develop a significant ecosystem. It is situated on what is termed a 'stress point' on the mid-Atlantic Ridge and on first acquaintance it seems that it has not much changed since its emergence from the sea. It has been described by Simon Winchester as: 'The earth in its raw state, unlovely and harsh, and grudging in in its attitude to the life that clings to it.'[6] In fact, it is now very different from the island that was first discovered, at least on its higher ground, although this has more to do with human intervention than it does with nature taking its own rather slower course.

When Darwin visited Ascension, he saw it largely as it had been left by nature, and was not much impressed. He found it 'very far inferior to St. Helena' and recorded the anecdote from a Mr Dring that Saint Helenians 'live on a rock, but the poor people at Ascension live on a cinder.' To Darwin, it had little to interest the naturalist: although unknown to him it retained a number of unique plant species, around eleven of which survive today. In fairness to Darwin, we should note that these have mostly been located and identified during the last thirty years. More may yet be found. As with Saint Helena, Darwin not only overlooked its native plants but remained

---

[6] *Outposts, Journeys to the Surviving Relics of the British Empire*, p. 123.

equally unaware of its endemic creatures. Understandably, he did not come across two species of shrimp, *Procaris ascensionis* and *Typhilatya rogersi*, which survive to this day in a single series of rockpools, a hundred metres from the sea, relying for their existence on sea water that reaches the pools through fissures in the intervening lava. These unique shrimps, in their tiny world, bring a whole new meaning to the word 'endangered'.

To Darwin, Ascension was a metaphor for hell, a place to torment terrestrial beings. He gave names to features on the island that they retain to this day, such as the Devil's Ashpit and the Devil's Riding School. But, in one respect, Ascension did have something to offer. Following an initiative by Darwin, it was destined to become a laboratory. An important experiment could be conducted here, and he left the island with this in his mind.

Darwin arrived back in England already acknowledged as a scientist of some stature. News of his fame had reached him at Ascension and he could now apply this to some purpose. He was soon in contact with his friend Joseph Hooker, son of the then director of Kew Gardens. Hooker was destined to become the greatest English botanist of the time. He took up Darwin's idea that a completely new ecosystem could be created on Ascension and moved it forward. The island lacked trees, for example, something that Darwin had noted. These could be provided both from Kew Gardens and from elsewhere in the fast-growing British Empire.

Hooker visited Ascension for the first time in 1843 and the experiment commenced in 1850, when three hundred and thirty plants were sent to Ascension from Kew Gardens. These were planted on the island's highest peak, now called Green Mountain. More species followed and by 1870 around five hundred alien trees had been planted. Some of these survived, an example of natural selection. What happened thereafter was extraordinary, as anybody ascending Green Mountain today can attest. A visitor now travels across the island from Georgetown through what remains a largely barren landscape, but then experiences a change, actually a series of changes, as the vegetation alters. Eventually, after a long series of hair pin bends in the narrow road up Green Mountain another world appears, a terraformed one. There are bananas, coffee trees, eucalyptus and other tropical plants growing at a height of almost three thousand feet above sea level, where once there were no trees or anything much else in the way of vegetation. A cloud forest has been created and moisture induced. There is insufficient evidence that extra rainfall has resulted, but mist interception is evident. The progress has been incremental and proceeds to this day. With more water there is more growth and with more growth there is more water.

Some will frown upon this, living as we do at a time when there is a great need to protect what is left of our natural environment. What of the island's endemics? What will be their fate? In fact, much of Ascension remains largely untouched by the experiment and, in any event, plants, including endemic ones, can be remarkably resilient. Where a new ecosystem is created, as has happened on Green Mountain, they may even adapt and further evolve. It is now known that some plants unique to the island have changed their habits as a result of human intervention in their environment. This is evolution in action, but on a much accelerated scale, as we have seen in Britain in recent years, where it has been shown that birds have developed longer beaks in order to benefit from the large numbers of birdfeeders that they now come across in our domestic gardens.

Ascension, and the Saint Helenian environmentalists who work there, have gained considerable attention in the scientific world in recent years. Sometimes this seeps through to the media. The BBC caught up with the story in 2010 when its science reporter, Howard Falcon-Lang, wrote: 'By a bizarre twist, this great imperial experiment may hold the key to the future colonisation of Mars.' *National Geographic* gave a similar spin to this in 2017, under the title: 'Mysterious Island Experiment Could Help Us Colonize Other Planets'. The *National Geographic* item featured Stedson Stroud, a Saint Helenian who was at that time responsible for the Green Mountain National Park. He retired to Saint Helena later that year. Stedson is well known in the world of conservation and has an MBE to show for his dedication to the environment on Ascension and elsewhere. Claire Fieseler, the writer of the article in *National Geographic*, suggested that he may well know more about Ascension's plant life than anyone else today. He certainly has the credentials. It was Stedson who found the last surviving examples of *Annogramma ascensionis* (the Ascension Island Parsley Fern) thought until then to be extinct. This gained international headlines in 2009 and brought much needed funding for conservation on the island. It also gained Stedson a place on an Ascension Island postage stamp, abseiling down a cliff in his trademark cap to find the now famous plant. Kew Gardens, in a reversal of what happened in Darwin and Hooker's day, has continued to play its part, with specimens sent there from the island being successfully propagated.

It could be argued that *Annogramma ascensionus* provides us with an example of why terraforming is not a good idea, at least as far as our environment here on earth is concerned. The plant's relentless path to near extinction may well have been due, at least in part, to competition from introduced species. Stedson, however, is one of life's optimists, and can put a positive slant on the created cloud forest. Plant species evolve over long periods of time if nature is allowed to follow its unhurried course, perhaps over millions of years. But, as with bird beaks in Britain, the actions of humans may change things rather more quickly, bringing accelerated evolution rather than extinction for endangered species. Such has been the case on Green Mountain. Some ferns that have happily spent many years living at ground level, in arid conditions, have migrated to damp mosses found on the trees, and are thriving there. They may well permanently adapt to this, as British birds have to birdfeeders.

As far as colonisation of other planets is concerned, the bigger question is that of humans. Whatever the adaptability of the plants that might sustain us there, can we do the same? We know that travel in space causes physical changes in astronauts, but this is generally a temporary phenomenon. An evolutionary process allowing us to live in space would not amount to much if permanent changes in our physical make-up were not possible. A recent flurry of interest in the media seemed at first sight to indicate that long term changes to our bodies might result from time spent in space. A comparison of identical twins, one of whom had been in space for 240 days, was reported in March 2018. Perhaps they were no longer identical twins. If true, however, a suggestion in the media of a difference of 7% in their DNA would have resulted in the arrival back on Earth of a new species: even chimpanzees, our closest living relatives, share over 96% of our DNA. That said, long term differences were detected in the physical make-up of the twins, but lifestyle on Earth, such as smoking, will produce similar results.

Over a very long period of time humans may well adapt to life on another planet, provided that they are able to live there at all. Which is where terraforming comes in. Having read the article in *National Geographic*, I asked Stedson Stroud, who I have abseiled down a cliff with in Saint Helena, albeit to get to a favourite fishing spot rather than to save an endangered endemic, what he thought about the prospects for colonising Mars. He does have something of a history in relation to space exploration: he once worked at the NASA Station on Ascension, making the coffee when the first Apollo radio transmissions were relayed from there in the 1960s, a fact revealed internationally by *National Geographic* in its article. Stedson is not offended by the description of his role and is upbeat about his contribution. When President John F Kennedy visited the Houston facility he is said to have asked a cleaner about his role there. 'I am helping to put a man on the moon' was the reply. Stedson adopts the same position, emphasising that the approach on Ascension was that everybody contributed in their own way. Coffee, he says, was important. It kept the technical staff awake as they worked the long hours required to make Kennedy's pledge of a man on the Moon by the end of the 1960s a reality.

As I steer Stedson away from the Moon landings towards the subject of settling Mars he suggests to me that it should be considered a much longer-term idea. The greening of Ascension may be a start but it will take a lot of caffeine to replicate this on Mars. For the moment, as Stedson emphasises, it remains the stuff of science fiction. To which we will now return.

Last and First Men: A Story of the Near and Far Future, by Olaf Stapledon, was published in 1930, to considerable acclaim. It offered the reader a story of the future history of humans, extending over a period of more than two million years. It includes some speculative genetic engineering, albeit a term that had not appeared at the time: it was first used by Jack Williamson in his science fiction novel *Dragon's Island* in 1951. Stapledon also wrote about the not yet named terraforming. In *Last and First Men* he put forward the idea of achieving this by producing oxygen from the oceans of Venus, using electrolysis.

Arthur C. Clarke later said that it was *Last and First Men* that most influenced his own writing. Clarke took up the challenge of terraforming in 1951, in his first published novel *The Sands of Mars*. In this, early colonisers of Mars keep secret from Earth the cultivation of plants intended to enrich the oxygen content of the Martian atmosphere: doing this in combination with 'Project Dawn', the ignition of a Martian moon named Phobos, thus providing the planet with its own supplementary sun. This moves forward the idea of adapting a planet so that humans living on it can breathe, early writers having assumed that a suitable one would simply be found.

Isaac Asimov progressed things with his novella *The Martian Way* the following year. In this, the reduction of shipments and threat of cessation of supplies of water to Mars from Earth leads to humans born on Mars towing fragments of ice back to their planet from Saturn's rings.

Perhaps the fullest treatment of terraforming in science fiction is Kim Stanley Robinson's Mars trilogy: *Red Mars* (1993), *Green Mars* (1994) and *Blue Mars* (1996). In *Red Mars*, a scientific research station, in effect a colony, is established by the 'first 100', as they continue to be termed throughout the trilogy. The settlers develop an environmental and social programme which changes both the planet and the Martians that the settlers become. As Arkady, one of the characters in the book, puts it, '…. we must terraform not only Mars, but ourselves.'[7] But terraforming the planet gives rise to ethical problems, which are soon addressed by Robinson through the dialogue in his book. What if any yet to be

---

[7] P. 113.

discovered life form is threatened? There is also the question of protocols established by the United Nations Assembly back on Earth. The counter argument to the idea of protecting endemic forms of life that may not even exist is that humans are the 'consciousness of the universe'[8], and are the only life form that matters. As a majority of the characters in *Red Planet* see it, the primary duty is to themselves, a philosophy that humans have more than amply demonstrated on Earth. In science fiction, as would almost certainly be the case if it became reality, humans do not much change their basic character as they explore the universe. On Mars, Robinson writes: '...no one wanted to live in a bath of mutagenic radiation, and the practical desire to make the planet safe for humans was stronger in most people than the desire to preserve the lifeless landscape already there, or to protect a postulated indigenous life that many scientists assured them did not exist.'[9] Unsurprisingly, terraforming wins the day. In *Green Mars*, as one might expect from its title, the adaptation of Mars to meet the needs of the introduced human population is well under way, with the 'red planet' having become a green one. By the end of *Blue Mars* there are rivers and oceans as well. The 'Martians', as they now are, have developed the ability through scientific advance to live considerably longer lives than humans left behind on Earth, a necessary device for ensuring that the continuity of characters is maintained throughout the trilogy, the time span required for the action of the three books being significantly longer than an earthly human's lifetime.

Robinson is an environmentalist, campaigning through the medium of science fiction. His treatment of such things as the complex nature of the soil in which we largely grow our food

[8] P. 213.
[9] P. 204.

shows us 'how much we take for granted in our everyday Earthly lives.'[10] The lesson is that we need to work at preventing ecological disaster here on Earth, which is very much Stedson Stroud's priority. He has the distinction of having rediscovered three plant forms previously considered to be extinct and being the first to identify two that were previously unknown to science: the *Cyperus stroudii* and *Acremonium stroudii* being named in recognition of this.

Perhaps work on Ascension will assist not so much in a colonisation of Mars as in improving the future prospects of human survival on our own planet; which, as it becomes increasingly precarious, is one of the justifications provided in *Red Mars* for terraforming Mars. Perhaps we can still achieve this on Earth without the need to experiment in other worlds.

---

[10] Adam Roberts, *The History of Science Fiction*, p. 458.

IX
Mason & Dixon

Charles Mason was born in April 1728 (the sole evidence of this being that he is recorded as having been baptised on 1 May that year). Jeremiah Dixon, whose birth is better documented, came into this world on 27 July 1733. They were destined to become an unlikely pairing: Mason being from rural Gloucestershire and Dixon from a coal mining background in County Durham. Mason made his mark early: by 1756 he was the assistant astronomer at Greenwich, serving under the Reverend James Bradley, the Astronomer Royal. In 1761 Mason was selected by the Royal Society to travel to Sumatra in order to observe the forthcoming transit of Venus, an astronomical event that it was considered would enable the distance between the Earth and the Sun to be determined: Dixon was to be his assistant in the enterprise.

In furtherance of their envisaged role Mason and Dixon left England on HMS *Seahorse* but were forced to return when a French frigate attacked the ship, leaving a number of the crew dead. Unsurprisingly, they were reluctant to set off again, but were persuaded to do so when the Royal Society threatened their livelihoods if they failed to continue with the project. As it was not then possible to reach Sumatra in time for the transit, they were instructed to carry out their task from the Cape of Good Hope. In the meantime, the Reverend Nevil Maskelyne had travelled to Saint Helena to observe the transit from there, along with Robert Waddington, a mathematician and fellow astronomer. Maskelyne was at that time curate of Chipping Barnet church, a few miles north of London. He later succeeded Bradley as Astronomer Royal, an advancement attributable at least in part to his work on the island, albeit that it had not been entirely successful in terms of the tasks set for him by the Royal Society.

These real characters and events are fictionalised in Thomas Pynchon's *Mason & Dixon*, published in 1997. The novel brings us to the era of what has been termed the 'evaporation of genres'.[1] *Mason & Dixon* has been described by *The New York Times* as a fusion of 'history and fable, science and science fiction.' It is a masterpiece and contains some of the best prose ever written about Saint Helena. Pynchon puts into words what it is like to be on the island, including the extraordinary feeling of how dominant, almost overwhelming, the sea is. Anybody who has ever walked or driven up through Half Tree Hollow, the overspill settlement of Jamestown, and has paused to look back, will have felt what Pynchon describes: 'For years, travelers have reported that the further up into the country one climbs, the more the sea appears to lie *above the Island*,– as if suspended,…'. The italics are Pynchon's.[2]

The Mason and Dixon of the title are not greatly remembered for their connection with Saint Helena, they are famous today for having surveyed and established the Mason Dixon Line in what is now the United States of America, but,

---

[1] Gary K Wolfe, *Evaporating Genres: Essays on Fantastic Literature*, cited by Roger Luckhurst in *Science Fiction: A literary History*.
[2] As is the American spelling.

for the moment, we must return to the South Atlantic. Following their enforced sojourn in Cape Town they travelled to Saint Helena and it is their time on the island which takes up much of the first part of Pynchon's book. In Saint Helena they meet up with Maskelyne. Like Halley, who as we have seen, was an earlier visitor to Saint Helena, Maskelyne received his early education in London, attending Westminster School, where his interest in astronomy began. His purpose in travelling to the island was, as with Mason and Dixon's work in Cape Town, to observe the 1761 transit of Venus. This was of considerable importance. Halley had been largely defeated by the weather in his observation of the transit of Mercury in 1677, an exercise, as with Maskelyne's, intended to enable the distance of the Sun from the Earth to be calculated. As Halley had proposed, following his own disappointment, the next best opportunity would be the transit of Venus in 1761, which occurred many years after his death. Along with his successful prediction of the return of what is now known as Halley's Comet, his posthumous fame largely relies on this.

A present day sign to Maskelyne's observatory on Saint Helena, near Hutt's Gate, shares its wooden post with the one pointing to Halley's. The sites pointed to are on different sides of the road, which runs from Jamestown to Longwood, and were equally unsuitable for their purpose. Although high up, the area is the wettest on the island and suffers significantly (as far as astronomy is concerned) from mists and low cloud. Halley had written of this: 'there was so strange a condensation or rather precipitation of the Vapours, that it was a great Impediment to my Celestial Observations.'[3] Unfortunately, when Governor Hutchinson was instructed to prepare for Maskelyne and Waddington's visit, his reply was:

---

[3] *Philosophical Transactions*, 1691, cited by Gribbin and Gribbin, p. 119.

'We have already erected an observatory for them in the country.' To be fair to Hutchinson, it is not obvious where the fault for this lies, Maskelyne had arrived on the island on 6 April and Hutchinson's letter is dated 21 May, so it may be that Maskelyne chose or at least approved the site. When it came to the observation of the transit of Venus on 6 July 1761, which was the main purpose of Maskelyne's visit to Saint Helena, the effort was largely defeated by similar conditions to those experienced by Halley. In his report to the Royal Society, Maskelyne was to write:

'The almost continual cloudiness of the skies, at the Island of St. Helena, renders it a very inconvenient place for the making of astronomical observations, which I had the mortification to experience in losing the sight of the exit of the planet Venus, from the sun's disc, on the 6th of June 1761, to observe which was the primary motive of my going thither.'

Ironically, the event was seen clearly from Jamestown, only a few miles away. Maskelyne later moved his equipment to a house in Jamestown, and wrote in his journal:

'Thursday September 24 I removed the clock down to James's Valley, and keeping the same length of the pendulum as before, fixed it up strongly against the wall of a house, in an upper room, whence I could make my observations through openings made in the roof of the house.'

Such is Saint Helena: an island on which a hole in a roof may serve better for an enterprise than an observatory built for the purpose. There is now little trace of Maskelyne's observatory: a modern house built on the promontory that it was once on is called 'Pleasant View', perhaps with a touch of irony.

Although the weather at Hutt's Gate thwarted the main purpose of his visit, Maskelyne's time on the island, together with his voyage there and back, did give him the opportunity to formulate his famous idea of determining longitude by reference to the position of the Moon, which became known as the lunar distance method: making use of the angular distance between another celestial object, the Sun or some other observable bright star, in the path of the relatively fast-moving Moon. Using a sextant, the measured angle between these two bodies enabled a navigator using tables calculated for the purpose to establish longitude. The method remained in use until the 1850s, when the development of the marine chronometer rendered it obsolete.[4]

Perhaps symbolically, in *Mason & Dixon*, it is the *Moon* that is Maskelyne's favourite drinking place. Jamestown was once a place of many pubs, now reduced to the *White Horse* and the *Standard*, but the names of many of the others have carried through to modern times, sometimes on the premises and sometimes simply in popular local speech. The period houses next to Saint James's Church, now turned into a hotel, are still referred to as the *First and Last*, a name derived from their proximity to the sea, hence being the first and last for mariners to enjoy on shore. The *Moon* remains, at least in name, in what is now Napoleon Street (Cock Hill in the book), which forks off from Main Street towards Longwood, a few yards downhill of its junction with Nosegay Lane, a delightful name which might easily have justified a mention in the book. The *Moon* now serves as the Bahá'í Centre and a gift shop called *Moonbeams*.

---

[4] Once accurate time could be kept at sea it was a simple matter to compare this with the time at a fixed point such as Greenwich and calculate longitude by reference to the difference between the two.

In Pynchon's account of Saint Helena, it becomes a colony in another world, an 'extra-terrestrial Plantation'. It is England's moon, settled by those who 'would never visit the Home Planet, alth'o some claim to have been there and back, and more than once.' This reflects the diversity of those who came to live on the island.

On a first reading, *Mason & Dixon* is not so much a novel as a series of accounts or episodes narrated by the Rev. Wicks Cherrycoke, a fictional parson supposedly familiar with the two main characters. Many of Cherrycoke's tales are capable of standing as stories in their own right, but taken as a whole they provide the continuity and structure necessary for the book to be a novel. Saint Helena is mostly featured in the first part of the book, *Latitudes and Departures*, which contains twenty-five of the numbered episodes. The action in the second part, *America*, largely takes place across the Atlantic, as its name suggests: but there are references within it to prior events in Saint Helena.

Ostensibly, *Mason & Dixon* is a history set in the period leading up to the American War of Independence. It is written in a language and style that mimics, perhaps parodies, the language and style of the time. The novel commences with Mason and Dixon exchanging letters and then meeting up with each other for the first time, following which they proceed to Portsmouth to await their departure for Sumatra. Here they come across a talking dog. It is difficult to know what to make of this. It sets the sort of challenge to the reader that is to follow throughout the book. Pynchon's novels are a bit like multiple choice questions that have no single correct answer, as is no doubt intended by Pynchon, the reader will make of it whatever he or she wishes, with all conclusions as to meaning being equally valid. It may be that the talking dog is simply a performing canine, kept by its owners for purposes of exhibition and profit, perhaps its apparent ability to speak is ventriloquised; alternatively, Mason and Dixon may simply be under the influence of drink. Perhaps there is a rational answer: Mason suggests that in the Age of Reason, 'There is ever an Explanation at hand, and no such thing as a Talking Dog – Talking Dogs belong with Dragons and Unicorns.' The dog, however, offers its own explanation. Dogs long ago worked out that humans have an abhorrence of eating the flesh of other humans, so they 'quickly learn'd to act as humanly as possible'. This strategy for avoiding being eaten was passed down, we are told, 'from Parents to Pups'. As the dog puts it, 'I am but an extreme Expression of this Process.' In short, he represents evolution. Whether the talking dog is an example of surreal fantasy, drunkenness on the part of Mason and Dixon or scientific explanation is a matter of choice for the reader.

When Mason and Dixon arrive in Saint Helena they meet up with Nevil Maskelyne, who is already haunted by a sense of failure. His observation of the transit, by contrast with Mason and Dixon's in Cape Town, had not gone well. His back-up position was the undertaking of observations of *Sirius*, which were adversely affected by equipment failure rather than the weather. The efficient working of his telescope depended on its plumb-line, which might seem to most of us to be an easy requirement, being simply a weight suspended on a line: but what might meet the requirements of a bricklayer does not necessarily satisfy an astronomer's more exacting needs. Pynchon has Mason and Dixon drinking with Maskelyne at the *Moon*, where Maskelyne is telling them of his difficulty with the plumb-line. He later explored this in considerable detail in his report to the Royal Society, which included that: 'The irregularities in question evidently arose from the friction of the plumb-line against the central pin; a fault, to which most of the sectors, made before mine, have probably been liable.' In short, it was not his fault but lessons had been learned.

Significantly, *Mason & Dixon* shares several science-fiction themes with Godwin's *The Man in the Moone*, which we may reasonably speculate that Pynchon came across in the extensive reading that he must have undertaken when writing his novel. One of the episodes in *Mason & Dixon* describes how two astronomers escape from an enemy by using a flying machine, as Gonsales does in *The Man in the Moone*. Cherrycoke narrates this as a story within a story. Mason and Dixon belatedly remember that an eclipse of the moon is due as they go about their work in America, resulting in a potentially expensive setback. In reliance on it being a moonlit night, bets have been placed on the outcome of a tree felling contest. A lawsuit over lost wagers beckons, there being suspicion among the losers that Mason and Dixon must have known there would be a lunar eclipse. A Captain Zhang offers the comfort that it might have been much worse for them in past times, when they could have been beheaded. This is the introduction to his tale 'of Hsi and Ho' which he recounts the next evening. Zhang tells Mason and Dixon that Hsi and Ho were astronomers to the Emperor of China. Their predictions, supplied to the Emperor were the source of the Emperor's power, who reveals them to his people as a sign of his own godlike prescience. The system breaks down when, like Mason and Dixon, the two astronomers fail to predict an eclipse of the moon. Their only option, other than certain death, is to escape, which they do in their flying machine. They take flight, quite literally, from their observatory, situated on 'a great Tower of imported Rajputana Marble'; achieved in 'a gigantick sky-blue Kite, of some strong yet light silk Stuff, strengthen'd with curious Bamboo Ribbing work, furnish'd with apparatus for steering.' The impression given is that it is the craft's maiden flight. Mason and Dixon are intended by Zhang to be as much uplifted by his story as Hsi and Ho are by their flying machine. In Zhang's account the flight ends with Hsi and Ho touching down in a lake, in the territory of another ruler who becomes their new employer. They now have the same work as they had before, but their predictions are fed to Lord Huang, which brings with it a considerably better outcome: Hsi and Ho are able to court Huang's daughters and eventually succeed to his lands.

It will be recalled that, in *The Man in the Moone*, Gonsales arrives in China on his return from the moon. It is from there that Gonsales sends the manuscript account of his adventure back to Spain, carried by historically identifiable Jesuit missionaries. There is a considerable Chinese/Jesuit connection in Pynchon, which also marries up with a major pre-occupation of Bishop Godwin's: it is telegraphy. In *Mason & Dixon* there is a conspiracy between the Jesuits and their Chinese converts in North America. According to Benjamin Franklin, the 'Jesuit Telegraph' has brought to perfection the 'Marvel of instant Communication.' This is clearly regarded as a threat, revealed by Franklin when he becomes the first Postmaster-General of the United States in 1775. In *Mason and Dixon* the detail of the process appears in Episode 53, where it is said that the Jesuits have found a way of using 'the Boreal Phenomenon to send Messages over the top of the World, to receiving-stations in the opposite Hemisphere.' There is a code, it seems, the basis for which is: 'Twenty-six letters, nine digits, blank space for zero.' We may reasonably assume this to be a joke on Pynchon's part, the twenty-six letters simply being those of the alphabet and the remaining part the digital technology we rely on today.

But what of Saint Helena? The island is different things to different people: to a mariner seeking safety and succour after the privations of a long voyage at sea it could be an earthly paradise; to a defeated emperor kept there against his will, a 'cursed rock'. As portrayed by Pynchon it is a dismal place where the winds can drive a man to distraction and severely test his sanity, perhaps pushing him over the brink. As Pynchon sees it, Maskelyne is one of those who has succumbed to lunacy. At Sandy Bay, on the windward side of the island, Maskelyne meets a soldier who asks him to seek the intervention of Clive of India, Maskelyne's brother-in-law, so that he can be released from service on the island. The island was an East India Company possession at that time and the soldier thinks only of a return to England: but he is a spectre, it is Maskelyne who hopes for release. The Saint Helena wind is haunting in its own right and features again in the American part of Cherrycoke's narrations, when Dixon expresses the hope: 'I pray the Western Slopes of Allegheny may prove less distressing than the Windward side of that wretched Island…'.

Towards the end of the book there is a return to Halley's legacy to science fiction of a hollow Earth, in which Mason and Dixon debate the theory: Mason playing the doubter and Dixon suggesting support. Dixon argues that 'creatures Microscopic' are to the human body what we are to 'the Planet Earth'. The point of this is that if we view things in proportional terms then we may have a better grasp of where we lie in the scheme of things. When Mason responds that there is 'no inner Surface' Dixon asks him, 'Have you been to its End, to see?' In the course of the exchange, Mason seeks an assurance from Dixon that he has not shared the idea, which appears to contradict Newtonian theory, with the Royal Society: their joint reputations are at stake. Later, Dixon visits the interior, unaccompanied by Mason. As he describes it, 'And 'twas so that we enter'd, by its great northern Portal, upon the inner Surface of the Earth.' Although clearly a fictional account, it is historical fact, a further excursion for purposes of astronomy, that allows Dixon to do this in Pynchon's novel. The 1761 observations of the transit of Venus having failed to provide a reliable calculation of the solar parallax the opportunity arose again in 1769, when it would have been night-time in Europe. It was then that Dixon participated in the effort, sponsored by the Royal Society, to take advantage of a further observable transit of Venus, a venture which took him to Norway on HMS *Emerald*, in the company of a Captain Douglas. Based on this, the third part of *Mason & Dixon* is called '*Last Transit*', dealing with the final years of the pair. Dixon tells Mason, who had turned down the offer of a place on the expedition to Norway, that the opportunity to visit the inner Earth had arisen on an island called Hammerfost. As described to Mason by Dixon:

'The Ice giving way to Tundra, we proceeded, ever downhill, into a not-quite-total darkness, the pressure of the air slowly, each sound soon taking on a whispering after-tone, as from a sort of immense composite Echo,– until we were well inside, hundreds of miles below the Outer Surface, having clung to what we now walked upon quite handily all the way, excepting that we arriv'd upside-down as bats in a belfry…'

There is much more in *Mason & Dixon*. The point is that the novel establishes a clear connection between Saint Helena and science fiction.

X

The Answer is 42

The Hitchhiker's Guide to the Galaxy started out as a radio series in the late 1970s and was later adapted for the stage, novels, film and more. It poked fun at science fiction and was required listening for a generation. Its hero Arthur Dent, the seemingly last surviving human, hitches a lift on a Vogon spacecraft following the destruction of Earth by the human-like Vogons, who were making way for a hyperspace bypass. Dent's travelling companion is Ford Prefect, an alien compiler of material for the guidebook of the title. The radio series was notable for its sound effects and for having been produced in stereo. What has proved to be the most enduring memory for many fans is that 42 was said to be the answer to 'the Ultimate Question of Life, the Universe and Everything', although this did not feature in the original radio series. A computer named Deep Thought calculates the answer, a random number that many have tried to read a deeper meaning into, perhaps demonstrating that science fiction can be taken too seriously at times. In the event, the answer amounts to nothing, with Deep Thought concluding that it is the question itself that needs clarification.

I did not expect to find that the number 42 was of any particular relevance in Saint Helena, but as this book was nearing completion, I walked into the Jamestown Museum where David Pryce, known on the island as 'the Bug Man', is a volunteer. Having heard that I was writing about the connection between Saint Helena and science fiction he offered to show me his car, a Land Rover Defender. Why? The answer was 42. Private vehicles on Saint Helena display only numbers on their registration plates. When a vehicle is scrapped, its registration number becomes available for re-issue. On applying to register his Land Rover, David enquired whether 42 was available: it was, and David became the proud owner of the number that so many science fiction fans would love to have.

There is, as well as David's Land Rover, much to be seen on the island that is connected with the theme of this book. As some readers are likely to visit the island and may even have bought their copy of the book there, I now offer a brief guide to other things that they may wish to look out for.

The fictional first flight on the island was from what is now Munden's Point to West Rocks. As viewed from the sea this would have been from left to right across James Bay. A visitor today is more likely to have arrived by air and will look across James Bay from its landward side, from behind the railings above the sea wall. From this position, Munden's Point will be seen to the right, with a number of structures visible on it. In its time it served as a battery and a place of detention. The path to it is not an easy one but is still open to those determined to get there. West Rocks are easier to access, but a visitor may be put off by their proximity to Jamestown's main sewage outlet.

To see the site of Halley's Observatory, which is several miles from Jamestown, a visitor should leave the town via Napoleon Street, which is the left fork at the top of Main Street, and follow the road towards Longwood. A few miles out of town, having gone past the track leading to Napoleon's tomb, the sign for the observatory can be seen, just before Hutt's Gate is reached. It is a fairly easy walk from the road to the site.

The same sign on the road also points to Maskelyne's observatory. There is no obvious path to this and the exact site has yet to be identified. A pile of stones to the left of the house now built there offers at least the possibility that these are the remnants of the observatory but there is no supporting evidence for this.

Maskelyne's favourite drinking spot, according to Pynchon's fiction, is in Jamestown, where the *Moon* may still be seen. I was fortunate to be shown around it by its present owner, Cliff Huxtable, and I queried the date of 1763 that is displayed on its exterior, this being somewhat unsympathetic to Pynchon's portrayal of Maskelyne, Mason and Dixon making use of it in 1761. Cliff assured me that there was nothing to fear, he had affixed the date himself when a visiting architect gave it as an approximate one for the *Moon*'s construction.

The various Napoleonic sites are well cared for and easily accessible, consisting primarily of the Briars Pavilion, Longwood House and the Tomb. The Briars Pavilion is the closest of the three to Jamestown, also being reached by following the sign to Longwood and starting out along Napoleon Street. Although now named after him, the former emperor passed along Napoleon Street only twice, the second time in his coffin. The Pavilion at the Briars, supplemented by a tent, was Napoleon's home for around two months while works were completed to make Longwood House habitable for him and his entourage. The Briars was at the time in the ownership of the Balcombe family: in 1956 it was re-purchased by a descendant and gifted to the French Government.

Continuing along the road towards Longwood House it is the Tomb that is reached first. Around three quarters of a mile from the road it offers a steep walk on the way back but for those able to undertake it the effort is amply repaid. It is a beautiful spot.

Longwood House is approached through the gatehouses marking the start of Longwood Avenue, one of the few straight roads on the island. In immaculate condition, the house now boasts both a gift shop and a café. Count Bertrand's House is opposite and is now a restaurant.

Porteous's House, in Jamestown, where Napoleon spent his first night on the island is long gone, but photographs of it survive. The building that has replaced it is not entirely sympathetic to its history. For those wishing to see it, it is situated by the entrance to the Public Gardens, opposite the recently renovated Mantis Hotel.

Mount Pleasant is a private house at Sandy Bay. In 1818 Napoleon stopped off for a picnic there: it was one of his rare excursions from Longwood. A letter of thanks to the then owner, Colonel William Doveton, in Napoleon's own hand, may be seen at the British Library in London.

Manuel Johnson's Ladder Hill Observatory now exists only as the piece of ground on which it once stood, with a plaque in the garden of nearby Bleak House pointing towards it. A few remnants of London yellow brick, which date from the Georgian era, are still to be seen on the site and may once have formed a part of the observatory's floor. The distinctive colour comes from the effect produced by the minerals in London clay when fired. Whole and broken London bricks are still found in various parts of the island and an example is on display in a glass case at the Mantis Hotel. Although the Ladder Hill Observatory itself does not survive, some of the equipment once housed there does, and may be seen at the

Museum and at Plantation House. The clocks are of particular interest. I was fortunate to be able to look at these in the company of Peter Williams, who maintains them. Peter, a retired motor mechanic with no specialist training in the maintenance of clocks, has an enviable ability to work out such things for himself. He is a practical man, making use of nylon cord and a variety of tiny tools that he keeps in an old fridge at his house. He told me how somebody before his time had balanced one of the clocks at Plantation House by placing razor blades on its weight. He demonstrated this by dropping a magnet attached to a piece of string into its casing, fishing out seventeen blades. Such is the ingenuity that flourishes on a small, remote island.

Stedson Stroud also typifies what can be achieved from a small island setting. He may not hold the secret to colonising Mars but he knows more than most about our native Earth. Having completed his education before he owned his first pair of shoes he went on to become an internationally acknowledged expert on conservation, specialising in previously unknown and endangered plant species. He rediscovered three that were previously believed to be extinct and found two that were entirely new to science. These last two are now, as we have already noted, named in his honour under the Linnaeus system of plant classification. He tells the delightful story of how he found a surviving example of the thought to be extinct Bastard Gumwood (*Commidendrum rotundifolium*) on Saint Helena. Coming from a long line of beekeepers he was pursuing a swarm in order to capture it for his hive. It led him to a cliff where he saw a tree of a type that he had never seen before. The rest of the tale would make some purist conservationists shudder. He and George Benjamin returned to the spot to investigate further. It was difficult to get to the tree and George suggested that Stedson get below it while he cut down an aloe stalk to prod it with. Stedson returned to George with the dislodged bits. Sent off to Kew Gardens these showed the tree to be a Bastard Gumwood. A further example was later found at Manatee Bay. It has been successfully propagated and a number of specimens have been re-introduced at suitable locations on the island.

XI
The First Flight

It is ironic that with a fictional flying machine having been built on Saint Helena as early as the sixteenth century it took so long for the first real one, other than helicopters from visiting ships, to actually touch down on the island. Godwin's *Man in the Moone*, although first published in 1638, tells of Gonsales building his 'engine' on the island in 1598 or 1599, but for more than four hundred years thereafter Saint Helena remained accessible only by sea. Taking the lack of air access into account it was until recently arguably the remotest inhabited island on Earth. Easter Island, in the Pacific, is further from any other land, but has had a scheduled air service since 1967, and Tristan da Cunha, for which a case may be made, is part of a group of islands.

The idea of an airport on Saint Helena was mooted from the mid-twentieth century onwards, including consideration being given by the South African Air Force to the building of a runway there in 1943. The United Kingdom Government announced plans for one in 2005, with a projected completion date in 2010, but this came to nothing. In 2011 a contract was finally signed for its construction. Basil Read, a South African company, was chosen and funding was provided by the United

Kingdom's Department for International Development. With the runway completed, calibration flights commenced in 2015 and the first fixed wing aircraft to land on the island touched down on 15 September of that year. The official opening of the airport was then scheduled for early 2016 but was delayed due to a problem that had not been foreseen: the turbulent conditions caused by what is known as 'wind shear'. This made it difficult to land aircraft of the size that had been envisaged: it had been intended to use a Boeing 737-800 in the provision of a commercial air service. In the event, this proved impractical and even dangerous. The first scheduled commercial flight, using a smaller aircraft, arrived at Saint Helena on 14 October 2017.

There has been much criticism of the final cost of the project, which was in excess of three hundred million pounds, and of the failure to open the airport on time. The description 'world's most useless airport' was applied to it by a number of United Kingdom newspapers and there were some who took delight in pointing out that details of wind shear at the site had been reported by Charles Darwin when he visited the island in 1836:

'One day I noticed a curious fact; standing on the edge of a plain terminated by a great cliff of about a thousand feet elevation, I saw at the distance of a few yards, right to windward, some tern struggling against a very strong breeze, whilst where I stood the air was quite calm. Approaching close to the brink I stretched out my arm, which immediately felt the full force of the wind. An invisible barrier of two yards wide, separated a strongly agitated from a perfectly calm air. The current meeting the bold face of the cliff must have been reflected upwards at a certain angle, beyond which there would be an eddy, or a calm.'[1]

Notwithstanding the Department for International Development's notable failure to give posthumous consultee status to Darwin, the construction of a runway and introduction of a commercial air service for Saint Helena is a major achievement

The technical challenges overcome in the building of the airport were astonishing. Prior to the project, anyone searching for a site for an airport on the island would have been hard put to identify any area of flat ground larger than the football pitch at its Prince Andrew School. Saint Helena consists of a number of mountain tops rising out of the ocean in the mid-Atlantic: these reach a height of two thousand six hundred and ninety-seven feet[2]. The island is largely surrounded by cliffs and there are only three places on it where a car can be taken down to sea level. Deep water immediately offshore precludes any idea of a runway projecting out to sea. To build an airport required that almost everything needed for it would have to come in by sea: to an island with no harbour, or any wharf at which a sufficiently large vessel could tie up to discharge its cargo.

The heavy equipment needed for the works was brought in to Rupert's Bay, at a new wharf built for the purpose. A road over seven miles in length was constructed from this to the airport site. More than half a million truckloads of infill material were used to produce a surface on which to build a runway, at a height of over a thousand feet above the nearby sea at Prosperous Bay. Perhaps the most surprising thing is not that it cost so much, that the facility failed to open on time, and

[1] Charles Darwin's *Beagle* Diary, ed. R.D. Keynes, p. 430.
[2] *Diana's Peak.*

that it has fallen short of expectations as to the size of the aircraft that can use it, but that it was accomplished at all. Saint Helena now has an air service, albeit that it was a long time in coming.

Bishop Godwin, writing in the early seventeenth century, gave us a fictional flight across James Bay, followed a few pages later by a flight to the Moon. Ironically, when it came to real events, putting a man on the Moon was achieved almost fifty years before it became possible to land an aircraft on Saint Helena.

Bibliography

Anonymous. 1775. A Voyage to the World in the Centre of the Earth. ECCO Print Editions.

Barger, Andrew. 2013. Mesaerion: The Best Science Fiction Stories 1800-1849. United States: Bottle Tree Books LLC.

Bates, Stephen. The Year of Waterloo: Britain in 1815.

Beech, Martin. 2015. Terraforming: The Creating of Habitable Worlds. Springer International Publishing Switzerland.

Behn, Aphra. 1995. The Rover and Other Plays. Edited by Jane Spencer. Oxford University Press.

Clarke, Arthur C. 1986. The Songs of Distant Earth. Ballantine Publishing Group.

Cormack, Lesley B. 1997. Charting an Empire: Geography at the English Universities, 1580 – 1620. University of Chicago Press.

Cressy, David. 2006. Early Modern Space Travel and the English Man in the Moon. American Historical Review.

Cross, Tony. 1980. St Helena: Including Ascension Island and Tristan da Cunha. David & Charles.

Crouch, Nathaniel. 1708. The English Acquisitions in Guinea and East India, etc.

Darwin, Charles. 1831 – 1836. Charles Darwin's Beagle Diary. Edited by R.D. Keynes. Cambridge University Press.

Godwin, Francis. 1996. The Man in the Moone. Introduction by Andy Johnson and Ron Shoesmith. Herefordshire: Logaston Press.

Godwin, Francis. 2009. The Man in the Moone. Edited by William Poole. Canada: Broadview Press.

Gosse. Philip. 1938. St Helena 1502 – 1938. Introduction by Trevor Hearl. Anthony Nelson.

Gribbin, John and Mary. 2017. Out of the Shadow of a Giant. London: William Collins.

Hakluyt, Richard. Richard Hakluyt and Travel Writing in Early Modern Europe. Edited by Daniel Carey and Claire Jowitt.

Hearl, Trevor. 2013. St. Helena Britannica: Studies in South Atlantic Island History, ed. A. H. Schulenburg. London, Society of Friends of St. Helena

Horne, Richard H. 1850. The Poor Artist: Or Seven Eye-Sights and One Object. London. Facsimile in Forgotten Books. London: FB &c Ltd.

Hues, Robert. 1552. Tractatus de Globis et Eorum Usu. Elibron Classics.

Jones, Steve. 2016. No Need for Geniuses: Revolutionary Science in the Age of the Guillotine. London: Little, Brown Group.

Leys, Simon. 1991. The Death of Napoleon. London: Quartet Books Limited.

Luckhurst, Roger. 2017. Science Fiction: A Literary History. London: The British Library.

Keay, John. 1991. The Honourable Company: A History of the English East India Company. Harper Collins.

Macdonald, John. 1790. Travels in Various Parts of Europe, Asia, and Africa, During a Series of Thirty tears and Upwards. Reprinted as Memoirs of an XVIII Century Footman, ed. John Beresford, 1927. London: George Routledge & Sons, Ltd.

Marryat, Frederick. 1839. The Phantom Ship. London: Henry Colburn.

North, Jonathan. 2016. The Napoleon Options: Alternate Decisions of the Napoleonic Wars.Frontline Books.

Ocampo, Emilio. 2009. The Emperor's Last Campaign. University of Alabama Press.

Pynchon, Thomas. 1997. Mason & Dixon. London: Jonathan Cape.

Roberts, Adam. The History of Science Fiction. 2016 (Second Edition). London: Palgrave Macmillan

Robinson, Kim Stanley. Red Mars. 2009 edition (first published 1992). London: Harper Collins.

Green Mars. 2009 edition (first published 1992). London: Harper Collins.

Blue Mars. 2009 edition (first published 1996). London: Harper Collins.

Royle, Stephen. 2007. The Company's Island. London and New York: I.B. Tauris & Co Ltd.

Scott, Sir Walter. 1827. The Life of Napoleon Buonaparte. Ed. Richard Michaelis. Gibson Square.

Selin, Shannon. 2014. Napoleon in America. Vancouver: Dry Wall Publishing.

Sobel, Dava. 1996. Longitude: The True Story of a Lone Genius Who Solved the Greatest Scientific Problem of His Time. 2011 ed., Harper Perennial.

Spencer Jane. 1995. Aphra Behn: The Rover and Other Plays. Oxford University Press.

Whitehouse, David. Journey to the Centre of the Earth: A Scientific Exploration into the Heart of Our Planet. 2015. Weidenfeld & Nicolson.

Wilson, William. 1851. A Little Earnest Book Upon a Great Old Subject. London: Darton and Co. Facsimile in Legacy Reprint Series. United States: Kessinger Publishing LLC.

Winchester, Simon. 2003 edition (first published 1985). Outposts: Journeys to the Surviving Relics of the British Empire. Penguin Books.

Wiseman, Richard. Shoot for the Moon. 2019. Quercus Editions Ltd.

Zirker, J. B. 2009. The Magnetic Universe. Baltimore: The John Hopkins University Press.

Printed in Great Britain
by Amazon